Also by Patricia L. Woodard
Twice Colombia

We're Waiting for You

Patricia L. Woodard

Edited
By
Kate Wernersbach

Order this book online at www.trafford.com
or email orders@trafford.com

Most Trafford titles are also available at major online book retailers.

Print information available on the last page.

ISBN: 978-1-4907-6451-1 (sc)
ISBN: 978-1-4907-6453-5 (hc)
ISBN: 978-1-4907-6452-8 (e)

Library of Congress Control Number: 2015913708

Trafford rev. 08/27/2015

 www.trafford.com
North America & international
toll-free: 1 888 232 4444 (USA & Canada)
fax: 812 355 4082

Contents

For all adoptive parents who acted with the purest of hearts. May you never lose sight of your shining star.

Introduction

When I started this book, I was certain it would fly from brain to computer to paper. My focus was so clear that I never imagined that before I could write "The End," the focus would change and that the original story would nearly disappear. The part that didn't change, however, was the part about my adopted son, Jamie, whose story inspired me to keep plugging away. What did change was accepting that this would not be a story about returning to Colombia to live permanently as I was so sure I would, but rather a story of acceptance, adjustment and reflection.

I continue my story, now, with parts of the Epilogue from the first book, *Twice Colombia*. The two stories are so intertwined that, after struggling to try another more creative approach, I accepted that references to previous events that are crucial to this story could best be explained by sharing some of the Epilogue again.

My sincere thanks to everyone who picks this up and follows the path of my Colombian circle, which, by the way, was not a clean-cut 360 degrees.

Epilogue

Bogotá, February 17, 2009...

My former roommate Dot and I are riding in a car in Bogotá with the Director of Colegio Nueva Granada's driver, José. He picks us up at the Hotel Bacata in *El Centro* at exactly 9:30 a.m. for a visit to the school and as we drive through the city on a cool, sunny morning, nothing is familiar. There are no landmarks that I recognize on the way up the mountain to the campus, except the view of the Andes in the distance. What used to be a winding mountain road that even taxis were hesitant to maneuver, is now a bustling four-lane highway passing directly in front of the gates to the school. Buses, taxis, and cars vie for space, and condominiums and office buildings surround the campus. There are certainly no young boys carrying cardboard on their skateboards, zipping around the hills in this area today. The city I knew of five million people in 1975 is now approaching a population of nine million and I wonder if I'll be able to accomplish my goal on this trip.

When I retired in 2004, one of my projects was to finally write a memoir about my year in Bogotá. I had started it many years earlier when I was thinking about the need to leave a record of my experience in Colombia for my son, Jamie, who was adopted there. I thought it was important for him to know something about his heritage other than what he heard on the news and read in the newspapers, and I wanted very much to help him preserve his cultural identity. So I thought that putting on paper what I remembered from my time in Colombia would help achieve that goal. Fortunately, my parents had saved the letters I wrote to them during those years, so I felt like I had a head start. With a full-time job (plus a part-time job occasionally), parenting, graduate school, and aging parents who deserved my time, however, the hours needed to work on a manuscript just weren't there. The years passed by with no first draft, and then, on April 1, 2001, the unthinkable happened. My adorable, funny, loving and challenging son became a homicide victim. With a single gunshot, my life, as I knew it, shattered, and my twenty-three year old son was no more. Time, and support from friends and family, helped me climb out of my hole of shock and despair, and gradually I started picking up the pieces of my life as I tried to make sense of this event.

I read the letters from Bogotá many times, but couldn't bring myself to read the ones from Cali, where I adopted Jamie. So that was how I started with the project: thinking about Bogotá because, by then, I was sure I wouldn't write about Cali. I felt that I had enough information to leave my nieces and nephews and other family members a record of a dream I pursued once. Perhaps one day they would enjoy reading about it, perhaps not. But it was important to me to examine my feelings about Colombia and come to terms with my attachment to the people and the country.

Through the Internet, I had stayed in touch with my Colombian friends and had even located Dot, my roommate in Bogotá. She had settled in Phoenix, Arizona, with her own adopted Colombian child, a daughter named Luci, married now and the mother of two. As I gathered my thoughts and letters for the memoir, I realized that what was missing was the memories that someone else might have which weren't mentioned in the letters to my parents – and surely there were many things I didn't put in the letters. I needed help jogging my memory! It was the fall of 2008, and Dot and I had not seen each other since 1976. With a few e-mails and phone calls, she agreed to a return trip to Bogotá and then a visit with my friends in Cali, and finally, a trip to Cartagena where she taught for a year. This was exactly what I needed and I knew she would be the perfect companion. My only regret was that I couldn't find my dear friend and companion Jerry, from my Bogotá days, because I knew he would have a lot to share.

We met at the airport in Miami on the evening before our early morning flight to Bogotá. After thirty-three years, we had no trouble recognizing each other and delved right into reminiscing about our time at Colegio Nueva Granada. For the next eleven days, she shared her memories, I shared mine and we laughed at how different they sometimes were. I had contacted the school before our arrival and was steered to the office of Alumni Affairs whose Director was Adriana Perez, a former student at CNG. She remembered Dot and me, but since she was not in our classes we, unfortunately, didn't remember her. Isabella Delgado, the Director's assistant, whom Dot and I both remembered, was the one who made arrangements for us to be picked up at the hotel by the driver for Dr. McCombs, the Director of the school. We found out that Charlotte Samper, a guidance counselor who was the daughter of Dr. Samper, the staff physician when we were there, was still working at the school. Also, Gustavo Vega, a math teacher, whom we both knew, had spent his entire career at CNG and was approaching retirement.

As José pulled into the gated driveway at school and waited for the guards to let us in, Dot and I took in the view and barely recognized the campus. There was an impressive brick entry and new buildings spilled in all directions, but the blooming flowers and lush foliage still defined the grounds. The main entrance into the administration area hadn't changed much, but the parking area had been moved. And the buses! When did they get this modern fleet of futuristic-looking vehicles? We surmised that the seats were cushioned and that there were probably bathrooms on board. With tinted windows, we guessed they were bullet-proof, as well.

We spent a lovely day with Adriana, our gracious host, and visited with Isabella, Charlotte, and even stopped by Gustavo's classroom to say hello. Our old classrooms were just as they were when we left, except the old blackboards had been replaced with the new, dry erasable ones. It was not hard to imagine that we had slipped back in time and that we were once again busy young teachers, working on lesson plans, waiting for the weekend to come so we could explore the city. The teachers we met that day could have been there when we were there and I felt an immediate connection to all of them. Dot and I wondered if they could see themselves in us as we talked to them about their experiences in Bogotá and explained our mission.

After lunch in the new cafeteria, Adriana asked if we would mind being videotaped during an interview she wanted to do with us for a book she was putting together on memories of CNG by alumni. We were happy to help out and had fun talking about what we had brought to the table as individual teachers. A theme developed around the idea of individualized instruction and we both realized, perhaps for the first time, that those efforts on our part were still a part of the program at CNG. Adriana thanked us for our contributions and acknowledged our commitment to the high quality and standards of the CNG community.

It was a worthwhile day and I came away from the visit with respect and admiration for the entire entity. Providing for the child, and encouraging excellence, leadership, scholarship and character still remained the guiding principles at the school. A new area of emphasis, service, had been implemented and I was thrilled to know that these privileged young people were now giving back to the community in many ways. The school itself had built a small separate school for underprivileged children and supported it with donations from the CNG families and alumni. I truly had moments when I wanted to ask if they needed any math teachers.

We noticed the delightful weather. Even on the school campus, I didn't feel the wind and it didn't seem to be as cold as I remembered. Someone told us that global warming had taken place there, just like everywhere, and while there was still plenty of rain in Bogotá, we didn't need our heavy turtleneck sweaters. There were very few people wearing *ruanas* and I regretted that, because that one article of clothing defined one of my most vivid visual memories of the city. We also found out that CNG is in the western part of the city, not the northern part, as both of us thought.

We visited a new upscale mall and quickly became aware of the armed guards around the entrances and especially in the area of the ATMs. All we could do was shake our heads in amazement that we were getting money from a machine in public, in Bogotá, while feeling grateful at the same time that the guards were there. Safety was still an issue and we never once let our guard down.

I was hoping to find the restaurant *Casa Vieja* where I had first eaten *ajiaco* and was disappointed to find out that there were now three *Casas Viejas* in the city. We had lunch at one that was close to the shopping center and the *ajiaco* was just as delectable as I remembered, but I couldn't rekindle a sense of having been there before.

We hired a driver at our hotel to take us around the city one day and he told us a lot about how Bogotá had changed. Chia, the little pueblo we used to visit about an hour from the city, was now a suburb of Bogotá with a major highway going straight there. Melgar, the quiet, secluded, weekend getaway at the bottom of a curving mountain road, where I spent so many weekends in the sun, had become a sprawling tourist mecca. A lot of land in that area, in and around the jungle, had been cleared to make way for new hotels and restaurants. I used to look at, and think about, the jungle often. We rode around the neighborhood of our old apartment, but the building was gone: in its place, another nondescript structure. Diego, our guide, pointed out the building where DAS, that scary and mysterious organization where we sat on the floor smoking cigarettes and drinking coffee on a cold, dreary day many years ago, is located. He also pointed out the American Embassy, where I had spent several difficult days twenty-three years earlier trying to get Jamie's visa, and none of it looked familiar. Demonstrations were going on at the time and Diego said, in that nonchalant way, "It's normal." He took us to a jewelry store and I bought a pair of small emerald earrings. I was curious to know if Oma's, the outdoor restaurant on *avenida quince*, where Paul and I spent many late nights with friends over coffee and cognac, was still there, but we couldn't find it. Only once did we see a donkey and wagon on a major street. We visited the old part of town where I was hoping to find the co-ops where we used to buy the local handicrafts, but only found stores that sold what appeared to be just the touristy items. I told myself they had to be there somewhere and if only I had more time, I'd find them. We revisited the Gold Museum, Simon Bolívar's home and the Botero Museum. *Empanadas* and fruits could still be bought from *kioskos* on the streets and people continued to move quickly as they went about their business – and nearly all seemed to be talking on cell phones. I remembered spending weeks without phone service when we lived here and couldn't imagine having access to the technology that was available in Colombia now.

Cali, February 20, 2009...

After a few days in the capital, we departed for Cali where I was looking forward to seeing my friends and making a visit to my old school, Colegio Bolívar. Many changes had taken place in my Colombian families and, while we had stayed in touch over the years, I hadn't seen any of them except Ximena's daughter, Margarita, who spent six weeks with me in the summer of 1996. Ximena, Rafael and Margarita had been in a very serious car accident in 1993 and were hospitalized for several months. Margarita, the least injured, and their other daughter, María Isabel, helped care for Ximena and Rafael during their recuperation. It was a difficult time for Ximena and her family as she and Rafael recovered.

María Isabel was a physical therapist and had married an orthopedic surgeon and together they opened their own treatment centers and expanded into several locations in the city. They now had two sons, Juan Miguel and José Tomás. Margarita graduated from college as an agricultural engineer and worked in the Colombian sugarcane industry. She was recently married and had one daughter, Salomé. They grew stronger as a family.

Unfortunately, Rafael's import business had suffered during the years along with the economy in Colombia, and times had been hard for them. Ximena had taken many jobs to help her family, and her faith and optimism remained strong. They lost many material things, but Ximena, of course, had become the backbone of the family and would guide them through challenging times until conditions improved. In addition, Nora, Ximena and Esteban's mother, and Chila, their aunt, had recently passed away. So, it was a period of much personal upheaval.

Since my last visit, in 1986, Esteban and Marta's daughter, Isabel, had grown up and was in her last year at the university. Soon she would be Dr. Isabel Plata, psychologist. Also, they had been blessed with a second daughter, Sofía, who was now ten years old. Esteban was still in the pizza business, supplying schools with daily pizzas, and had opened a restaurant and hotel in Lake Calima where they finally built their vacation home with an expansive view of the lake. Most touchingly, Marta had survived breast cancer and had recently finished chemotherapy treatments. Her prognosis was excellent and she was gradually getting her strength and her hair back.

But one thing had improved for all of them. Nearly everybody now had washing machines, which, in many cases, eliminated the need for live-in maids. The many young girls and women, who, in the past, were destined to a life of domestic work, were now looking for opportunities in other areas. The economy was changing, and with presidential elections coming in a year, there was a sense of optimism.

Without a thought about themselves and any misfortunes they may have experienced, my Colombian family welcomed me back with love and open arms. Of course they knew about Jamie and spoke freely and openly about him. Their approach was good for me and I was encouraged to say anything I wanted. They asked a lot of questions, but never passed judgment on my decisions. Their support was solid and I was happy to be with them.

Their generosity extended to being our driver and tour guide the next few days and our first trip was to the school with Esteban and Isabel, called Isa. It seemed impossible that nearly twenty-five years had passed since I eagerly embraced an eighteen month experience that would have such a meaningful impact on my life. As we approached the school, I noticed there was a lot more traffic than I remembered and that the *Blanco y Negro* buses, upon which I had relied heavily, looked tired and worn out. They were soon to be replaced by a new transit system, called *el Mío*. Once through the security gate and parked, we headed to the office of Carolina Chavez, Alumni Director. I marveled that the grounds of the campus were as green and lush as ever and how the relentless heat seemed to magically disappear when we stepped in the shade. The new buildings looked as if they had always been there.

The auditorium where I spent so much time in the spring of 1984 seemed to resonate with the sounds I remembered from "South Pacific," and I could clearly see and hear in my mind "Bloody Mary" and "Some Enchanted Evening" being performed.

The new outdoor eating area made me think of a room upstairs where faculty and staff would go for breaks and meals, and the day I sat down in a chair only to have it collapse as I sprawled, unhurt, on the floor. New furniture soon arrived.

I remembered the students lounging on the grass during lunchtime, eating *empanadas* and a strange kind of hot dog that had cheese inside, usually followed by a quick siesta.

We walked to the pool area and I thought about how impressed I was when I first saw it. The idea of having access to a pool like that on a daily basis was thrilling and I made use of it frequently – especially on the weekends when we were allowed on campus. It's where I took Jamie the first day we went out together.

The soccer field was just as I remembered except on this day there were no students playing a match. Yet, I could still see them in my mind, charging up and down the field with the fans cheering and having fun on the sidelines.

The new state-of-the-art library and computer center took my breath away. In 1984, if I remember correctly, there was one classroom that had a few computers which were, I think, TRS-80s. I don't know if there was an actual computer class at that time, but Russell Bloom, in charge of that operation, could often be heard moaning and groaning when the electricity flickered and all work was lost. In those early days of computer experimentation, there were some brave souls who took on the task of moving the school into a computer-savvy environment. Now, in 2009, it was obvious they achieved it. This new library was named in honor of Dr. Martin Felton, who was Director when I was there.

We walked to my old classroom and I was eager to experience again the unique sensation of teaching in a room with three walls and a panoramic view of Colombia at its best: the mountains in the distance, the grass which still made me want to go barefooted, and the students who brought so much joy to my life. They were focused, intelligent, friendly, curious, and lively and could they ever dance! I remember the day one of them said, "Ms. Woodard, look, there's your son!" And there his class was, romping across the grass with their homemade "horses."

I caught a glimpse of Alain Bouchard and even had a chance to speak briefly with Manuelita Velasco, both teachers when I was there. Dr. Felton had retired and was living in Cali. Sadly, one of his daughters had died in a tragic plane crash just outside of Cali in 1995. I was delighted to meet his other daughter who was now teaching in the kinder program at Colegio Bolívar.

We ended our tour of the school with Carolina, who graciously took the time to help me recall some precious memories and also to witness the new exciting times unfolding now. My life had definitely been enriched by being a part of Colegio Bolívar, and I was greatly moved by this opportunity to revisit a very special time in my life.

Before leaving, Carolina said, "Patricia, we're planning a big reunion June 12, 2010, for the alumni. Why don't you come?"

I hadn't thought of returning to Cali so soon but thought, "Why not?"

"Thank you, Carolina. Keep me posted. I'd love to come back."

For the next few days, my friends entertained us and kept us busy. Esteban, Marta, Sofía, their friend Yolanda, and Dot and I went to Lake Calima for the weekend and we stayed in their home overlooking the lake. When I asked if they ever went to the river any more they replied, "Now we come to the lake since we have the house. We come nearly every weekend. For us the house is a blessing." The house was right beside Esteban's restaurant and cabins which his brother, Nacho, took care of during the week. While at the lake, we also went by María Isabel's vacation house, called *la casa azul*, the blue house, because it was painted a vibrant shade of blue reminiscent of Frida Kahlo's blue house in Mexico. We had wine, cheese and crackers before going for a boat ride and visit with Esteban's brother Ismael and his wife, Patty. At night we rode into a little town, Darien, and walked around the square and ate *arepas*. Sleep came easily on those cool nights.

Back in Cali, we visited the new zoo, went shopping and rode by my former apartment building, *Las Torres de Santiago de Cali*. We walked around the new mall with Xavier and Esteban following at a discreet, but protective, distance behind the women in our group. We ate papayas, mangos, empanadas, and had lunch one day at an Italian restaurant, Salerno's. María Isabel picked us up one afternoon and took us to her gorgeous apartment where we enjoyed coffee and sweet muffins. Dot, of course, had never met my friends in Cali, and was greatly impressed by their hospitality and generosity. Since she was my friend, she was their friend; I think she understood my connection to all of them.

On our last day in Cali, Esteban drove us to the airport. We were saying goodbye, thank you, and doing a lot of hugging, while promising to send pictures soon. Suddenly, Esteban said, "Patricia, we love you! Come back soon!"

"I love you, too! And I'll be back!"

Cartagena, February 25, 2009

Our last stop on the Colombian trip was Cartagena and by the time we got there, we were getting tired. A beautiful, historic city on the coast, it was new to me, but Dot had taught there one year and wanted to revisit the school, which sat on some prime real estate right on the beach. We hired a driver and visited the school where Dot found information about one local colleague she had known many years ago. She was able to make contact with her and paid her a short visit.

We spent a couple of nights in a charming hotel in the old section of town and walked late in the afternoons. Hot, humid and tropical, people disappeared from the streets during the hottest part of the day, but came out aggressively when the breezes picked up and the temperature cooled off. An international film festival was in its second day when we arrived so there were a lot of tourists in town – interesting people just to look at! I nearly stepped in *mierda* several times on the narrow sidewalks and decided I needed to come back to Cartagena when I was in a better frame of mind. My patience was depleted and I was ready to get home.

My objective on this trip had been to jog my memory back into the mind-set I'd had nearly thirty-five years earlier. I hoped that spending time with Dot in Bogotá and trying to recall those times would give me the insight I needed to pursue my memoir. And also, I wanted to visit Cali and my friends there to see if I should think about the possibility of returning on a more permanent basis. Mission accomplished on both counts! I was ready to write and, yes, Cali was calling me.

Chapter One

Testing the Waters

When I left Colombia in February, 2009, after a much anticipated trip, I felt a new awakening. I was comfortable with my relationship with my memories and the thought of returning again to that beloved country permanently was just a seed. Nourished and tended, that thought quickly developed into another visit to Cali, in June, 2010, under the guise of attending the class reunion at Colegio Bolívar. I had remained in contact with Carolina Chavez, director of Alumni Affairs at the school, and she assured me I would be welcome and could bring someone with me to the celebration. I was thrilled to think I might actually see some former students and colleagues.

Another objective in making the trip was to look at apartments since I knew there was a real possibility I might return to Colombia. I wanted to get a good handle on what to expect in terms of expenses in case I decided to move forward with the idea. Since I would not be going as an employee of the school this time, settling in without that support could be a challenge. What about the visa? Health insurance? Transportation? Banking? Yoga classes? Could I sell my house in New Bern during a period of a weak and struggling economy? There were many things to think about, and fortunately, my longtime friends, the Platas and Francos seemed eager to help. I added new questions and concerns to my "to do and think about" list almost daily and realized quickly that this move would be different from the other two times when I left home for extended stays in Colombia. For those two trips, my parents were still living and I had depended on them for many things: first, the use of their house as a place to store items, and second, the use of their mailing address for forwarded mail. Sounding simple and almost insignificant to a younger person, those matters became complicated with age, and would have to be resolved.

And I was beginning to see another side to acting on the urge to live in a foreign culture. Although Colombia no longer seemed foreign in the way it did in 1975, I knew that moving there again would mean I'd have to face many obstacles which didn't exist earlier. In addition to not being employed, I'd now be facing retirement as a senior citizen. That could be challenging enough in one's own familiar surroundings. While I loved being retired and I flourished in my life away from the routine of a five-day-a-week job, could I find that same satisfaction in Colombia? Would I need a roommate? Would it be safe to live alone? What about a car? Always independent, it was important to me to know that I could take care of myself and, so far, I had been able to do that. But, I had to be reasonable.

My former roommate in Bogotá, Dot, had traveled with me to Colombia in 2009, but I decided to go alone this time since there were so many things I needed to do. This would be a fast trip, one week, and my focus was to concentrate on the possibility of returning to Cali as a resident, not just to vacation. I don't think anyone would have enjoyed traveling with me under those circumstances.

When friends Esteban and Marta Plata found out my plans, they insisted I stay with them instead of a hotel. I was prepared to stay at *Hostal Santa Rita*, where I had stayed the year before, but they were adamant. Esteban said he wanted his daughters, Isabel (Isa), and Sofía, to know what it was like to have me stay in their apartment, since he and Marta had been my hosts during the Friendship Force trip in 1982. They thought it would be a valuable experience for their daughters to see how people who speak different languages from different cultures can communicate and get along. So, again I was the recipient of the generosity and kindness of friends, and I accepted their invitation to stay in their apartment in Cali.

During the fifteen months between the two trips, Isa, now in college and close to graduation, and I communicated through e-mails since her English was very good. Esteban and Marta sent messages through her, and of course, Ximena, Esteban's sister and my dear friend, and I continued to correspond – she in Spanish and I in English. We never had problems understanding each other.

Significant events had occurred in my personal life during those fifteen months as well: my mother passed away in August 2009, cutting a final tie that was painful. I was left feeling empty, but inspired by the example of her life. My own life now took on a new clarity and focus. I made progress with my memoir *Twice Colombia* and hoped to publish it within six months. In fact, before leaving for Colombia in June, I delivered the first installment to my editor. I quietly started planning to put my house on the market because I knew I couldn't afford to move to Colombia and keep the house. It was the worst possible time to think about entering the real estate market but I methodically forged ahead with plans to get the house ready.

Colombia was on the verge of a new presidential election and the favored candidate, Juan Miguel Santos, was promising to continue with efforts to achieve peace through democratic measures, if not, perhaps, peace with the guerillas. In fact, for the first time in recent history, only one of the six candidates had direct ties to the guerillas and Colombian citizens were excited about the prospect of a free and peaceful election. My Colombian friends had great hopes for the future and I shared that aspiration with them. I was soon on my way.

Chapter Two

Tank Tops and Perfume

With shiny black hair swinging and high heels clicking, the young women bustling around the Miami International Airport on June 8, 2010, were concrete evidence that I was headed to South America. Wearing jeans, tank tops and smelling of expensive perfumes, they were easy to identify with their distinctive air and verve. Even women of a "certain age" (and there was no denying that I had to put myself in that category now) had a style and flair which set them apart from other women. Very few of the women wore comfortable walking shoes and I recalled that whenever Colombian women were in public, generally they were dressed up and wore full makeup. I wondered if they still wore high heels by the swimming pools. I was thrilled to see a few people in the airport wearing *ruanas* (Colombian capes or ponchos); it was mostly older people, and I knew they were headed to Bogotá or some other place cooled by the frigid air high in the Andes. The men seemed to all be dressed the same: jeans or casual slacks, t-shirts or short-sleeved cotton shirts, and a sweater or jacket here and there, just like men back home. So, here at this international crossroad, I gradually felt myself willingly transition to the land of *El Dorado* and couldn't wait to set foot on Colombian soil again.

There were no surprises on the Avianca flight from Miami to Cali. A three and one-half hour trip, I looked forward to the hospitality and service which were always abundant and for which the airline was famous. As I settled into my aisle seat, I immediately noticed the clean, modern amenities and examined my individual TV monitor carefully: a nine-inch LCD screen, remote control, USB port, power socket, headphones, along with a coat hook and cup holder. Who could have imagined these things back in 1975 when I moved to Colombia the first time? Even now, many people in the States still think of Colombia as a dangerous, third-world country, lacking in sophistication and technological achievements. Not true. People crossed themselves, as I expected they would, and we taxied down the runway. Within minutes after takeoff, the steward delivered magazines. Soon afterwards, he brought us hot towels to wash our hands and five minutes later they were quietly picked up. We were offered pillows and blankets (free of charge) and soon settled down with free beverages, including the delectable Chilean wines. Our free dinner came later and consisted of typical airplane fare, but somehow seemed tastier and fresher than stateside meals which we usually had to pay for on flights. That night we had tender baked chicken with an unknown sauce, creamed potatoes, and a salad of lettuce, tomato, cheese, and Italian dressing, along with a roll. And, of course, all the wine, coffee or soft drinks we wanted. Dessert was lemon cake with a creamy icing sprinkled with coconut. There was nothing to complain about late that evening.

At some point during the flight, about an hour before landing, one of the bathrooms in tourist class was declared out of order. That meant that the wait to use the restrooms was longer than usual and I decided to get in line before I had an emergency. While inching my way to the back, I started talking to one of the stewards and soon he offered all of us in line a glass of wine for the inconvenience (they were actually six ounce cups into which four ounces were poured.) We gladly accepted his offer and laughingly asked each other if anybody had ever been offered free wine on a flight in the States. By the time we landed in Cali at Alfonso Bonilla Aragon airport on that summer night, I was happy, excited and looking forward to seeing my Colombian family.

Chapter Three

Return to Cali, 2010

Househunting

After passing through Customs quickly and easily, I stepped out into the velvety mist of the Colombian night and quickly spotted Esteban, Marta, and their two daughters, Isa and Sofía. I rolled my suitcase behind the rope and navigated a path through the crowd as my Colombian friends approached me with smiles, hugs and welcomes. Esteban eagerly took my suitcase and we were soon in the car and on our way through the verdant and rural countryside to Cali. Laughing and talking (in our own fashion) all the way, the previous fifteen months dissolved and, again, I knew I was where I was supposed to be.

The Plata's apartment was in the northern *barrio* (neighborhood) of Chipichape. I loved the sound of that word and found out on the previous trip that it really has no meaning – just a word that belongs to Cali and the Cauca Valley. In addition to several apartment buildings, the *barrio* also includes the upscale and modern Chipichape mall and Carrefour, of the French grocery store chain. I was looking forward to being in an area where I could walk alone safely, and perhaps consider living there myself. "This just might be the place," I thought.

When we pulled into the driveway to their apartment building, the door to the underground garage opened and Esteban carefully and skillfully eased the car into one of their two parking spaces. Their apartment was on the fourth floor and consisted of three bedrooms, two and a half baths, living/dining room, office/den area, a spacious balcony and maid's quarters. Isa and Sofía, who ordinarily slept in their own bedrooms, were bunking together during my visit so that I might have a private bedroom.

Before going to bed, I had a small glass of juice and we all turned in. Sofía had school the next day, Isa had her work at her new school, and Esteban and Marta had their day planned.

The girls were gone by the time I got up the next morning, and Marta was at the gym. Since her cancer scare a few years ago, she had embraced an exercise regime that included three trips a week to the gym. She looked healthy and strong and seemed to be in complete remission. I planned to go with her to the gym one day since she preferred the one owned by María Isabel, Ximena and Rafael's daughter, and I was curious about the available options. Finding out about yoga classes was also on my list.

As soon as I finished breakfast, Esteban said, "Patricia, do you want to look at some apartments before we run some errands? There is a new apartment building going up at the end of this block and I think we can get in to see one of the models."

"I'd love to, thank you," I replied, thrilled to have this opportunity so soon. Esteban knew I was interested in making a permanent move to Cali and that I wanted to see some available properties.

Soon we were on the construction site wearing hard hats, walking up stairs to look at a one bedroom furnished unit. Stage 1 of the development was scheduled to be completed by August of 2010 and stage 2 by February 2011. The building was twelve stories high and would include one bedroom studio apartments, and two and three bedroom apartments, ranging in size from 580 sq. ft. to 1266 sq. ft. Modern, strategically located, and stylish with many amenities, Miró, (the name of the complex), also included two elevators, lobby, sauna, Jacuzzi, Turkish bath, social room, outdoor kitchen for barbecues, Sky Club on the top floor, and a pool for adults. Of course, 24-hour security was on the property. Each apartment also had a deck and some of them opened to a view of the mountains – others, however, faced a blistering afternoon sun.

We were met at the door by a young woman who showed us around and answered our questions. The studio apartment we were in was small, but very modern and up-to-date. The first thing I noticed was the kitchen which, in typical Colombian fashion, had just one sink. I had always found washing and rinsing dishes in the same sink awkward but had managed to make it work in the past. Dishwashers had not yet arrived in Colombia. With very little counter space, a microwave oven would probably need its own table. There was barely enough room for a blender and coffee pot, the two appliances that most Colombians now had. There was a washer-dryer hookup. The floors were tile, but the sales agent, Malory, said if I bought an apartment, I would have a choice of tile or laminate flooring. Laminate flooring was one of the latest fashions there, but I felt without a doubt that tile was better in that climate. The bedroom had built-in storage in the closet and the bathroom had updated lighting features with a pedestal sink and glass enclosed shower. All of the furniture in this unit was sleek, and in the European style, and complimented well the sophisticated color choices for the interior of red, black and white or brown, black and white.

When Malory, Esteban and I sat down to talk about the details, Malory gave us papers with information about the different sizes, estimated completion dates and prices. A maid appeared with *tinto,* the strong black Colombian coffee, heavily sweetened with sugar. An apartment this size was approximately ninety thousand dollars or eighty-five thousand cash. I had always heard that negotiations were expected. That sounded reasonable to me, but I knew I couldn't buy anything until my house sold and that was still in the future. I couldn't imagine living in such a tiny space anyway, but I was willing to consider all possibilities. So, after looking at everything in detail I realized that I preferred something similar to Marta and Esteban's apartment. And I also decided, at that point, that when my house did sell, I'd be better off renting for a while, and then I could make a decision about buying, or not.

We left Miró and crossed town on the way to pick up Isa at one of the three schools where she was working. Many changes had taken place in recent years regarding public education in Colombia, and pre-kinder classes were now available for most children. Isa worked as a psychologist at three schools in the downtown area, *El Centro*, and traveled among all three each day. There were 37 students in the school we visited and they all wore uniforms of shorts and t-shirts which the government provided. Three and four years old, they appeared happy, healthy, and excited to have visitors. When Isa introduced me and asked me to say something in English, the children broke out in uncontrollable, hysterical laughter. I wasn't quite sure what they were laughing at, but I hoped it was a good sign. We took some pictures and then they sang for us. It was gratifying to see the advances being made in public education, and I remembered the previously common sight of children, who should have been in school, on the streets, begging for food and money. Isa told me that those children were still around, but their numbers had dwindled considerably. In fact, my adopted son Jamie had been one of those children. This time, I did not see any outstretched hands. I agreed with many that the key to peace in Colombia would start with education for all.

After the visit we returned to the apartment for lunch which the maid had prepared. It was a soup of chicken broth with potatoes, a chicken and rice dish with peas and carrots, sliced tomatoes, bright red and at least four inches in diameter, and *lulo* juice. As always, the meal was satisfying and tasty and my hosts were gracious. Esteban told me that the maid came only three days a week for eight hours a day and was paid approximately twelve dollars a week. I thought about the full-time, live-in maid we had in Bogotá in 1975 and the standard rate of twenty dollars a month which we paid her. The arrival of the washing machine in Colombia had made a huge impact on the need for domestic help, and of course, there had been changes in the economy. I wondered what I would need when I moved into my own apartment and knew it would be a different world than what I had known in Bogotá and Cali many years ago.

After a siesta for all of us, Isa and I walked across the street to the mall and the grocery store Carrefour. We looked at everything in the French-owned chain store, and I checked for aluminum foil, low fat milk, and other low fat or reduced fat products, all things that had, at times, been hard to find in Colombia. The fruits and vegetables made me salivate, and I examined the fresh herbs carefully. I thought I'd probably be able to find anything I wanted.

Over the years I had cultivated my own herbs, but most of them were seasonal, and during the winter, I had to rely on grocery stores for my supply. Finding such an abundance of them now and knowing they would be available year round, quelled fears of having to eat canned and processed food, or rice and potatoes as part of a steady diet, out of necessity. This time, everything I wanted and needed seemed to be there. In addition, there were canned soups and many new processed foods, which were tasty, of course, and of which the Colombians seemed to be very proud, but which I had gradually removed from my diet. I remembered so well my dad saying, in 1975, when I told him about life in Colombia, "That's the way things were here fifty years ago." And for all these years, I tended to think about that when some new product became available in Colombia and I knew that he was right. The processed food was a prime example.

After looking at everything, we left Carrefour and walked next door to the Chipichape mall. The stores here were modern, and some, exclusive. This is not where the lower classes shopped. Isa and I stopped at Zara's, a fashionable, upscale boutique whose parent company is in Spain, and I found a pretty, blue, cotton blouse for a reasonable price. Using my credit card from the States was simple – all I had to show was my driver's license, and I made my purchase with no problems. From there, we walked around the mall and looked at all the stores while waiting to meet Marta and Sofía. I made a quick stop at an ATM machine to get some pesos. The Platas were planning to attend an out-of-town wedding the coming weekend and were looking for a dress for Sofía. We soon caught up with them and all of us had input into Sofía's choice. While we were in the store, Esteban sat on a bench outside the store, but still in eye-sight, and read the newspaper. Such was a family shopping excursion in Cali.

When that was taken care of, Marta, Isa and I left in Marta's car and went to Catorce, a Colombian grocery store chain that my friends favored. Esteban and Sofía left together in his car and went to pick up Carolina, Sofía's friend, before meeting us again at a *panadería* (bakery) on the way home. Catorce was smaller than Carrefour and had been around a long time. I understood the preference for a familiar place to buy groceries. While they were buying their things, I picked up some coffee, *Bemoka*, to take back to the States, vitamin pills, (they actually had my brand!), and a Chilean wine to share with the family. Parking was tight, right on the street, and when we left, Marta gave the attendant a tip for watching the car. He also guided her as she pulled back into traffic. I mentally made a note of this and realized that if I bought a car in Colombia, I'd be dealing with this kind of traffic on a daily basis.

From Catorce, we headed to the bakery, where we enjoyed *pan de bono*, warm and fresh from the oven and one of my favorite Colombian specialties, and washed it down with juice and *café con leche* (closer to milk with coffee than coffee with milk). After eating and resting, we were soon rejuvenated and ready to tackle the rest of the evening. We headed back to the apartment where Sofía and Carolina worked on a school project and I tried to organize some things in my room. The girls put their posters and markers and supplies on a table on the balcony and before long, Marta was directing the activity. Esteban even had some input when he suggested a different color combination. It was a family affair which was typical on school nights.

One of my gifts to the family was a children's book written by a friend of mine, Judy Stead, titled, *The Twelve Days of Christmas in North Carolina*. In addition to writing the story, Judy also did the colorful and fanciful illustrations. At some point during the evening, we looked at the book, read some (it was in English), and took some pictures.

When the project was finished, the book finished, and the girls had gone to bed, Marta, Esteban and I talked about the Friendship Force trip in 1982. I had brought a copy of my pocket calendar from that time and was trying to fill in some gaps about our activities during those two weeks. My book, *Twice Colombia,* was progressing and I was now working on the second half of the story, which takes place in Cali. We marveled at the fact that their children were not even born then and that our friendship had survived for such a long time from such a long distance – and most of that time we didn't have access to the Internet! When we finally turned in, I was happy and at peace, grateful for these dear friends. I was more determined than ever to try to convey this aspect of life in Colombia, which even some of my own family members didn't accept, in my book. We had a lot in common. Sleep came easily.

In addition to looking at apartments during this week, I was also hoping to find information about, and perhaps attend, a yoga class. Yoga and walking had become my favorite physical activities back home and I didn't want to give up either one. As if on cue, Marta had arranged for us to go to María Isabel's fitness center early the next morning where I could attend a yoga class and she could do her exercise routine. The small class ended up being for María Isabel and me, plus the instructor who rode into the basement garage on her motorcycle. It was a strenuous, one hour workout with a strong emphasis on the sun salutation. The music she chose was more Indian flavored than that used by my teacher in the States, with lots of bells, sitars and vocals, and I enjoyed the variety. So that was one more thing I could check off my list. Yoga was available.

We returned to the apartment after our class to a breakfast of papaya, freshly squeezed orange juice, bread, cheese and coffee – American style for me, *café con leche* for Marta and Esteban. We talked about the special visa I would need to live in Colombia and Esteban made a call to a friend who worked at DAS, the government agency that had been so mysterious and frightening when I lived in Bogotá. The friend recommended that I get the special visa for retired people at the Colombian Consulate in Miami or Washington. He said it could usually be done in two months and was not difficult for someone in my situation to get. He didn't anticipate any problems. DAS!!! Real people! I was in awe that Esteban could make contact so easily. But my previous experience with DAS led me not to get my hopes up too quickly.

By that time, the sun was shining, the maids were bustling around the apartments, and everyone was going about their daily activities. The girls had been gone a long time to school and work. I could hear street vendors announcing their own arrival and watched from the balcony as the maids left the apartments and went outside to purchase flowers and avocados. Other maids were hosing down steps in front of the apartments and brick masons were busy repairing walkways. Gardeners were trimming shrubbery. From the fourth floor balcony, I could also see the mall, Chipichape, and noted that the parking lot was filling up quickly. Cars, buses and motorcycles were on the move. People were jogging or walking, and in some cases, women were alone. That gave me a ray of hope since I often liked to walk alone and was concerned that, in Cali, I may not be able to move around easily or safely without a companion. As the noise level increased, and salsa music crept in, I looked in the other direction and caught a glimpse of the mountains, losing their early morning mist – drawing me in, like a magnet, to find my place.

When Isa arrived home from work, early in the afternoon, Esteban told us we should look at another apartment that was available in the southern part of the city. It was owned by an American woman who was planning to return to the States, and being familiar with the property, he thought I would like it. It was at least a forty minute drive from their house, but he thought I needed to see other options and he had already called to let the owner know we were coming.

Isa, who drove with an earbud plugged in her ear for her phone, made and answered calls while driving, and was a surprisingly safe and careful driver. Even the motorcycles, which appeared to outnumber the cars, didn't seem to faze her, but they bothered me. At that time of day, the afternoon traffic was heavy, and I didn't know if I even *wanted* to drive in Cali.

After a long ride through the city, we pulled off a major thoroughfare and drove into a quiet residential area. I noticed there were no grocery stores or shops within walking distance. Isa drove to a simple three-story building and parked the car in front. I couldn't tell if there was protected parking for the residents and that would be a real consideration if I chose this apartment. It still wasn't safe to leave cars on the streets overnight. We locked the car carefully, removed all items from the seats, and approached the gate which had a speaker for guests. The owner of the apartment, her name was Patricia also, was expecting us and had given the guard permission for us to enter.

Her apartment was on the third floor, the penthouse. The lobby, stairwell, and surroundings were clean, airy, and full of light. The tile floors appeared to have just been mopped and were glistening. We chose to walk up the stairs instead of taking the elevator and were met at the door by Patricia.

"Hello, welcome, and please come in," Patricia said, greeting us like old friends. She knew Isa and her family, but not me. With short blond hair and an eager demeanor, she ushered us in as Isa introduced us. I didn't think she was Colombian, but she definitely had a Spanish accent when she spoke English.

"So, Patricia, you are thinking of moving to Cali and you're looking for an apartment?" she asked.

"Yes, Patricia, I'm considering making a move but right now I'm trying to get a feel for the available apartments. This is a lovely space."

I could hear birds chirping and could feel a light breeze wafting through the open and spacious rooms. Patricia informed me that her daughter and her family lived in Texas and she thought it was time to move closer to them. She had been selling her furniture and told me I could have anything she had left if I wanted it.

"You can even have the same telephone and number." I noticed a big screen TV and she said "I'm not taking any of this with me." The TV was much nicer that the one I had at home and the other furnishings were more than adequate. Her draperies were custom-made and came with the apartment. They would have been a big expense for anyone trying to set up housekeeping here from scratch. The kitchen boasted small gas and electric stoves which I really liked because of the frequency of power outages. I had the same back-up plan in my own house at home and having access to both came in handy many times. I could see myself preparing meals on the colorful and spacious tile counters. The three bedrooms and three baths were clean and roomy. But the most outstanding feature was the wrap-around balcony which surrounded three-fourths of the entire apartment. Filled with plants, unique pottery, a few pieces of furniture, including a hammock, it beckoned one to sit down and enjoy a cool drink and a cool breeze. Five birdcages were located in a covered area and she said she would have to leave the birds, too.

"What are you asking for the apartment, Patricia?" I asked, knowing I wasn't in the market to buy something until my own house sold, but curious anyway.

"Seventy thousand dollars" she replied, "and I would need it in cash, in dollars."

It was probably a good thing my house had not sold and that the money was not in the bank because I was as tempted as I'd ever been to make an offer. Even with no parking and no stores within easy walking distance, I wanted the property. And I knew that, regardless of what I eventually chose, I'd have to make some concessions on my wish list. Fortunately, I realized quickly that I wasn't ready to commit to a purchase of this size by writing her a check. In addition, I rationalized, the apartment was a long way from my friends in the North and I was hoping to be closer to them. Make no mistake about this, though: that particular apartment spoke to me, and under different circumstances, it would have been mine.

We chatted a while longer and soon were on our way to Chiquitines, the orphanage where I adopted my son Jamie.

Jamie - The Early Years

He was a funny little boy. Not weird funny, but ha-ha, make you smile and laugh funny. Before he could speak English, he would approach complete strangers and make them cackle by talking as if they understood everything he was saying. He was so engaging that no one ever indicated they were annoyed by his sometimes goofy antics. On his first trip to the barber shop after we came back to the States, Jamie quickly asked the barber, in very broken English, if he had ever cut off anyone's ear. The barber, along with the other customers, looked at him and chuckled, and then the elderly gentleman very calmly said, "Not yet." Jamie's eyes nearly doubled in size as he took that in.

In his early school years, he was somewhat of a novelty to his classmates with his foreign tongue and exotic background. He was smart enough to play that up and loved the special attention he received when he smiled and grinned, and flirted, really, with the young girls. His teachers weren't immune to his charms either. In the beginning, when he was just a little fellow, that was not much of a problem, but in time, as he grew and developed into a handsome young man, his ways turned manipulative. It was hard to believe that such a cute, adorable little boy could be devious, but I knew his background and I had had contact with other children in Colombia who came from his earlier environment, mainly on the streets. They could beg and plead and delight, all at the same time, and more often than not, eventually get whatever they were after. So, Jamie had learned this behavior at an early age.

When he finally arrived in the States, in May 1986, after our being separated for nearly ten months, we had to reacquaint. We had just spent a week together, first in Cali and then in Bogotá, where we picked up his visa and made final arrangements for the trip back to New Bern. Holding my breath for the entire trip, I was surprised that he was so easy to travel with. On previous flights he'd had a tendency to go to the bathroom a lot, walk up and down the aisles, and wiggle around in his seat and play. He didn't demand much of anything this time, however, and seemed to sense that this trip was finally going to take us "home." What a lesson in faith and perseverance, for both of us.

It wasn't until we passed through Immigration in Miami, where he somehow managed to knock over a styrofoam cup on the desk of the officer who interviewed us, and then stood on his head while I was filling out papers, that he lit up like a firecracker and let loose. His little body seemed to erupt with a force I hadn't witnessed before. He danced, jumped around, and grinned with such joy and happiness that I forgot that he couldn't really grasp what had just transpired in his life. Being on US soil now meant he was here to stay and there would be no more disappointments in getting him out of Colombia. Fortunately, we had a lot of walking to do in the airport that day and burning up that pent-up energy helped calm him down for the final part of our trip.

We settled into the small condominium I had purchased in Riverbend prior to moving to Colombia in 1984. On the first night in our home, I showed Jamie his bedroom with new pajamas laid out on his bed, and the bathroom we would share. He immediately jumped up and grabbed the shower curtain rod to swing Tarzan-style over the bathtub. Fortunately, when he and the rod with shower curtain attached, plunged to the floor, he was only stunned. I was in shock.

It was the middle of May and with only a couple of weeks left in the school year, he entered first grade speaking almost no English. What he had learned of the language while we were together in Cali seemed to have disappeared. I went back to work and made arrangements for him to be picked up at school in the afternoon and taken to daycare until I could pick him up. This arrangement worked well for the remainder of the year when we could finally enjoy our vacation together. He appeared to be a happy child and showed no signs of stress until his teacher contacted me at work one day and left a message that he apparently had a toothache. My sister Rachel, who also worked for the school system, was able to pick him up and take him to my dentist, Dr. Leslie Ipock, who agreed to see him even though he wasn't a children's dentist. By the time I arrived at his office, Jamie was curled up in a reclining chair, looking scared, but not terrified. He tried to smile and struggled to be brave. After an examination, Dr. Ipock identified an infected tooth and proceeded to treat it. While he was doing that, I was standing right beside Jamie, trying to console him and doing my best to make him comfortable. A few minutes into the procedure Jamie suddenly let out a big fart, right in Dr. Ipock's face, that nearly knocked both of us out. I was beyond embarrassed, but suddenly the three of us all laughed, and Jamie got through his first trip to the dentist here in the States with no harm done.

A year and a half earlier, I had taken him for his first dental examination in Cali and the dentist had discovered fourteen cavities. Over a period of several weeks, the dentist took care of all of them, and eventually gave Jamie a clean bill of dental health. I soon took him for his first visit with a children's dentist in New Bern, but I always appreciated Dr. Ipock's care and concern. He never failed to ask about him when I went in for my own check-ups and we usually shared a good laugh as we remembered Jamie's visit.

Early in the summer, I received a letter from friends in Cali who said they were moving to the States and wondered if they could send their son, Teos, ahead to stay with me while they were winding up business in Cali. Betty and Edgar Abadía, former colleagues at Colegio Bolívar, were considering New Bern as a permanent home and wanted to visit, along with Betty's aunt Hilda who lived with them. I was not enthusiastic about having houseguests for a big part of the summer, but remembered the interest and support they had shown when I adopted Jamie in Cali and didn't feel I could say no. My hopes were that it would not be for a long time because I knew that

Jamie and I needed a lot of bonding time before returning to school in the fall.

Jamie and I picked up Teos at the airport in Raleigh and Betty, Edgar and Hilda had plans to come at a later date. After getting Teos settled in Jamie's room and setting up a cot for Jamie in my room, we went about establishing our routine. Breakfast, lunch and dinner at a certain time each day with each boy having responsibilities. Jamie needed help in sticking to the routine and occasionally balked, but he gradually accepted his obligations.

We went to the beach several times and talked about pirates. Both boys had an interest in the swashbuckling characters. They looked for booty on the beach and chased crabs. On Jamie's first trip to the seashore, what he wanted to do most was bury himself in the sand and then have me take a picture. I have no idea where he saw someone doing this, but wherever it was, it made a real impression. So I helped bury him up to his neck and then took a picture. He kept that picture for a long time. We took the ferry from Hammock's Beach State Park to Bear Island and he was thrilled skimming across the open water. I was concerned that he might still be afraid of the water, but he wasn't. It would be a short while before he was swimming on his own, but it happened quickly once we started swimming in the pool at Riverbend, where our condo was located. Soon he was swimming alone and diving from the diving board.

We enjoyed other activities around town, but each time I received a letter from Betty and Edgard, I secretly wished there would be news about their arrival. I had hoped so much that Jamie and I could spend time together, just the two of us, before school started in the fall, but it was difficult to do with a guest in the house who needed, and deserved, my attention. Teos, about five years older than Jamie, was fluent in English and Spanish, and that helped a lot with communication among the three of us. At times, Teos was able to explain things to Jamie that I couldn't, and I will always be grateful to him for his help.

He was a kind and considerate boy. But, after a while, he was still a guest and I was beginning to feel my own personal stress with the crowded, unsettled living situation. At a time when I was trying to replenish my savings account, feeding and caring for another person was making a dent in that effort. When he and Jamie started squabbling, I knew it was time to explore other solutions.

Letters from Betty indicated that the time of their arrival was still unknown, but that they hoped it wouldn't be much longer. We decided together that letting Teos visit his aunt in Los Angeles until Betty and Edgard were settled in New Bern would be a good idea. They could then send for him. It turned out to be a great move because it gave Jamie and me a few precious days to be alone. Within a week of Teos' departure, however, Betty, Edgard and Hilda arrived. Betty and Edgar slept on pallets in the living room, Hilda in Jamie's room, and Jamie came back to my room. Any thoughts I had of spending time with my boyfriend fell by the wayside and that relationship was put on hold and soon came to an end.

"Patricia," Betty said one morning. "Would you mind if we borrowed your car one day so I can go for an interview for a teaching position? It shouldn't take long."

Knowing they were handicapped without a car and no real public transportation in the area, I said "Of course. Just let me know as soon as you can when you need it and we'll make some plans."

A couple of days later they drove to a neighboring county that was about an hour away. On the way back they stopped for gas and for some reason forgot to put the gas cap back on. They didn't realize it was missing until they got home and by that time the cap, whether it was left on top of the car or some other place, was long gone. They were extremely apologetic, but didn't offer to buy a new one. The money they had brought from Colombia was going fast, they said, and I didn't insist that they buy another one. However, my money was tight, too, and I was not happy about having to buy another gas cap.

Eventually they found jobs, bought a used car, and moved into a small, furnished condominium. They sent for Teos and the four of them settled in while waiting for their belongings from Colombia to arrive. My first day back at work was the day they moved out, but I didn't go back with enthusiasm and a positive frame of mind. I wasn't close to being ready for a new school year. To be honest, I was tired before the year even started. Jamie, however, was excited to return to his friends and new experiences, and for that I was grateful. I was learning a lot about making sacrifices and being a parent and that lesson would continue for a long time.

The following year brought Jamie and me some happy times. He celebrated his birthday for the first time here in September, his first Thanksgiving and Christmas, and he came to know his loving grandparents and other family members. They all doted on him in the beginning and our calendar was full. When it snowed the first time, he was out the door in a flash to build a snowman. On Saturday nights we often watched television after cooking something special, and he soon developed a liking for the show *Golden Girls*. I'm sure he couldn't understand all of it, but he connected with the ladies and laughed as hard as any fan. Saturday night was also when we danced a lot. It didn't matter what the music was as long as it had a good beat. We rocked and he went to bed a happy child.

We visited my aunt and uncle, Berniece and Harry Dunnagan, at their home in Myrtle Beach, S.C. and also their vacation home in Blowing Rock. On the trip to the mountains, I arranged a horseback-riding outing for one morning. I don't think Jamie had ever ridden so I watched him carefully as we mounted our horses and prepared for a group ride. He was enthusiastic about riding but I was afraid that the pure size of the animal would frighten him. Not a chance. After watching him a while, the instructor said he was a natural. In fact, he was much more comfortable than I in the saddle. On another mountain trip, we went whitewater rafting and he absolutely had no fear. We loved these outdoor activities and always had fun.

Jamie's early years were probably very typical of a middle class boy being raised by a working, single parent who wanted to provide a loving home for her only child. There were scouts, soccer, basketball, summer camps, and always time with friends and extended family. Trips to the beach were a part of our lives and we soon started flying kites there when the weather was cool. When it was time to get rid of our Christmas tree, we took it to the beach and placed it with others to help with soil erosion. Schoolwork and projects increased as the years passed, and Jamie's English improved quickly. When behavior problems surfaced, they were dealt with and all I could hope for was that I handled the situations in an appropriate and meaningful manner.

The first time I was aware that Jamie had stolen something after he arrived in the States was at a restaurant in New Bern that had a tempting display of candy at the register. My sister Rachel joined us for dinner one night at Friday's Seafood Restaurant, and after we finished and paid the bill, we walked to the car. Jamie sat between Rachel and me in the front seat, and as he was getting settled, some candy fell out of the pocket in his jacket.

"Jamie, where did you get that?" knowing immediately that he had lifted it from the display case while I was paying the bill. He looked at me with a sheepish smile on his face and said nothing.

"Okay, we have to take it back," I said. We walked back into the restaurant and spoke to the cashier. At that time, Jamie was speaking very little English, but he understood "I'm sorry" and he also understood that taking things that didn't belong to him was wrong. After being prompted, he apologized, and the young woman accepted his apology. When we got back in the car, we had another discussion about stealing. Even though I knew he wasn't understanding everything I said, I felt that with enough reinforcement, he would eventually absorb the message. I sensed that this behavior would be difficult for him to change and that premise held true for his remaining years.

Soon after that incident, Jamie asked me one day if he could use a needle and thread. When I asked him why he wanted those things, he said he tore his shirt. I looked at the shirt, and sure enough, there was a rip in the seam. I threaded a needle and gave it to him. Later, I came across his jacket and found that he had fashioned pockets out of some scrap material and was sewing them to the inside of the jacket. He had seen this in Cali and planned to stash his contraband in the pockets. Again, we had a long discussion about stealing and I did my best to keep him busy with other activities.

Jamie's first snowman.

Summer camp at Riverbend. Jamie is on
the front row, second from left.

Up a tree in New Bern.

Early drawing by Jamie, made after a visit to Blowing
Rock in the mountains of North Carolina.

Chiquitines

When friends found out I was considering a return to Colombia on a permanent basis, a common reaction was "Are you sure you want to do this? Won't it be painful?" as if I were in denial about my son Jamie's birthplace and the tragic details of his death. Perhaps they thought I would be masochistic to subject myself to daily reminders of his loss or perhaps they thought I wanted to indulge in self-pity. None of that could have been further from the truth.

Colombia, for me, was a connection to a happy and promising time in my life: a time full of hope, accomplishment, and, clearly, fulfillment. After all, this was where Jamie, that scrawny, undernourished little fellow first came into my life. This was where I developed life-long friendships with people who have brought much love, value, and support into my life.

So, considering a return to Colombia was a way for me to explore my feelings about the happiness and contentment I had felt when I lived there. I didn't know what made up the layers of my existence there, but I knew that great tragedy had followed great joy and that an injury that wouldn't heal was still a source of much personal pain. Perhaps, I reasoned, cherishing the happiness I once had should be enough, but it had become increasingly important to examine my feelings. There were many questions for me to try to answer as I started this quest and an important step was to revisit Chiquitines, the orphanage where Jamie had been taken that day in September, 1984, when he was rounded up with other children who were roaming the streets of Cali.

I had wanted to visit the new facility on this trip for a number of reasons. First, I had never seen it – it was built a year after Jamie's adoption – and I was curious. Second, I wanted to talk to the Director about making a donation, and third, I needed to renew my connection to the source of perhaps the most profound event in my life. I hoped it would strengthen my belief that his adoption was not in vain.

Isa had called the orphanage the day before to arrange an appointment with Agatha León, the current Director of Chiquitines. Remembering the other orphanage, the two-story colonial house which had been a private residence before becoming an orphanage, I vividly recalled walking onto the property the first time: the huge oak tree in front, surrounded by old tires where the children played, the protective walls topped with broken glass, the playground area, the covered verandah, and the mental picture I had of the children being hosed down after a trip to the river. And clearest of all, I could recall the small, inner office where I sat many days with Sra. Carvajal, as we discussed the adoption.

The new building was a one-story brick structure, modern and well-cared for, surrounded by a well-manicured lawn. Tile floors and large open windows with afternoon breezes wafting through greeted us as we walked in and identified ourselves. There were several tired-looking women doing what appeared to be routine office work at computers. Stacks of papers covered their desks and I could only imagine the number of hopeful parents waiting for their applications to be processed.

We were soon taken to Sra. León's office and she immediately insisted that we call her Agatha. A charming, bright, attractive woman who had attended Colegio Bolívar, she spent the next hour describing the financial support the orphanage received and the function of the orphanage at this time. They currently housed approximately forty-five children and most of them were under the age of four. Older children were cared for in other facilities in the country. She gave me information about making a donation and how to transfer money from the States. When that was all taken care of, we then took a tour of the grounds.

We passed a room close to Agatha's office where vertical shelves were full of files containing applications from past adoptions.

"Patricia, your original papers are here, too," she said. "At the time you adopted Jamie, we weren't using computers so the first application you filled out is still here – along with the notarized copies of legal papers, references, medical reports, home study, everything! Now, much of our work is saved on the computer."

I was momentarily shocked to think that such a huge chunk of my life could be found right here, on these shelves. There was a fleeting moment when I considered asking her if I could see my file, but quickly realized there was nothing to be gained by doing that and simply said, "Incredible."

From that room we passed through the building as Agatha pointed out the spaces for donated toys and clothes, the quarters where the children slept and ate, and the infirmary. There was a large room for infants, and several adult women were tending to the babies who were squalling and making baby noises. A few of the children were in car seats on the walkway and we stopped to coo at them and touch their fingers. They appeared healthy and happy. Then we saw the older children outside in the playground area. When they saw Agatha and Isa and me, they came running and nearly knocked us down with their enthusiasm. We hugged them and chatted with them, as much as we could.

Suddenly, Agatha said, "Patricia, this is Lulu, she worked at Chiquitines when you adopted Jamie. Lulu, do you remember Jamie?" It would have been remarkable if she had said yes after twenty five years, but it didn't matter. We looked intently at each other and I showed her a picture of Jamie which was taken when he lived at Chiquitines. She smiled sweetly, but did not acknowledge recognition.

"Do you mind if Isa takes a picture of you and me together, Lulu?" I asked. She nodded, and we stood together while Isa snapped a photo of the two of us.

I was happy to see the children so well taken care of and to know that adoptions were taking place on a regular basis. With a satisfied and grateful heart, I said goodbye to the children and staff and walked with Isa to our car. As we pulled out of the parking lot, I took one last look at Chiquitines and saw a little boy, standing alone on a grassy knoll, hand raised to his mouth, looking at us. From a distance he looked just like Jamie. What would life hold for him, I wondered, and I refused to let myself think beyond that.

Jamie – Signs of Change

In the intervening years, Jamie's behavior became a serious issue. He could still be loving and helpful and easy going, but his tendency to challenge my authority became more pronounced. He was fairly well-behaved until he was crossed, and during those times he was very outspoken. I never felt threatened by Jamie during this time, but he did once get angry with me for trying to set some limits on his behavior, and said, "You can't tell me what to do. I'll punch you in the face." He began stealing things from me and family members, and when confronted, denied it or was unremorseful. At first, it was small things, like inexpensive costume jewelry or small amounts of change he would find on my dresser. He gave the jewelry to his girlfriend(s). I was able to get some of it back, but not all. One valuable piece of jewelry that he took was my mother's engagement ring which had been a gift to me years earlier. The family of the girl he gave it to moved to another town before I could retrieve it, and I never saw it again. My sister who lived in Whiteville discovered one of her rings, which had been a gift from her husband, missing after we had visited one weekend. Jamie denied taking it, but there was always that suspicion. Later, when drugs became an issue, he stole larger and more valuable items such as my camera and word processor which he pawned. Items began to show up at home which I didn't recognize as things I had bought. By the time he was twelve years old, I realized he was sneaking out late at night in order to get together with friends who were older. This was the year his grades began to drop in school, and when he was sent to detention hall a number of times.

He broke into my sister's house when she was away one time and took a string of pearls which had been a gift from my parents. We had visited with her the day before this happened and the way he got in was by unlocking the window in the bathroom and unhooking the screen while we were there. The next day, while she was at work, he, along with a cohort, went to the house, walked around to the back, removed the screen and opened the window. The string of pearls was by far the most valuable item they took. During this time, Jamie had learned how to record on a cassette recorder, and before Rachel discovered the pearls missing, Jamie recorded a tape for her, confessing he had taken the jewelry. Apparently consumed with guilt, he gave her the tape and she immediately called me. I listened to the tape and was horrified that he had taken such blatant advantage of her generosity. When I confronted him he explained to me how they got in the house and who the other boy was. I found out where the boy lived, and went immediately to his house, hoping to recover the pearls. Jamie always claimed that this boy was the one who took the jewelry. When I got to their trailer, the boy and his mother were at home. The boy denied everything and the mother just took a step back and let the boy talk. We never found the pearls. By this time, Rachel felt she had to file charges. She had always supported him and had lavished attention on him, but it was now time to try another tactic.

As a juvenile and first offender, Jamie was placed on probation. I requested a psychological evaluation through his school and after receiving the report, I realized he needed more help than I could offer. I contacted an attorney and decided to apply for his admission to the Boys and Girls Homes (BGH) of North Carolina in Lake Waccamaw, which was close to Whiteville where my mother lived. They offered a safe and secure environment to children who, for whatever reason, needed an opportunity to begin the healing process. There was a strong emphasis on developing positive relationships, rediscovering academic success and preparing for the challenges of adulthood. Conflict resolution, time management, personal responsibility and character development were also a big part of their program. There were many success stories of young people who had passed through their program. When

Jamie was accepted, at age twelve, I was greatly relieved, but at the same time, saddened that he would not be with me. I knew that it was the right thing to do and I also knew that just hoping his behavior would improve would not accomplish anything. He needed skilled, professional help.

If he had any qualms about going, he never let on. I am convinced that he truly had a conscience that weighed heavily on his soul and I think he really wanted to change the way his life was going. I think he also knew that he was loved and supported. During his stay at what we called the Boys Home, he seemed to fit in and respond to the special attention he was receiving. His school work was completely acceptable and the regular reports I received indicated he was making progress. The social workers and counselors who met with him always had glowing reports and predicted that he would function in a totally responsible manner when he became an adult. One worker indicated that if any child ever deserved a second chance, it was Jamie. Sometimes these reports concerned me because I knew how he could charm people when he wanted to, and I hoped I was wrong in thinking he was being manipulative.

Another psychologist who met with Jamie several times, reported that he appeared to be "a rather lonely, deeply insecure young man who felt somewhat adrift, cut off from a source of nurturance and caring." There was talk for the first time about his "very real depression, low self-esteem, and difficulty expressing his feelings in a modulated and constructive fashion." Jamie was apparently open with this doctor. He expressed a strong desire to be home with me while still acknowledging that his time at Boys Home was an opportunity for him to get much needed help with his behavioral problems. It was pointed out that "his voiced interest in overcoming his behavioral patterns is a very positive sign; however, it must be remembered quite realistically that it will take time to accomplish significant changes."

Jamie took part in the many activities the Home provided and seemed to enjoy them. Perhaps his favorite one was caring for the animals on the farm where much of their food was grown. He eventually won a blue ribbon and trophy in a 4-H contest for the strongest and best-looking pig in a competition and seemed to thrive on the outdoor, physical activities required of him. With no soccer team to play on, he took up running and won several contests.

All seemed to be going well and I was anticipating that he would stay there the recommended amount of time of at least two years. When I or my mother visited him, he was sweet and loving. Since she was only ten miles away, she would often visit him and he became very attached to her. Mother was always supportive and I knew that he looked forward to seeing her. Occasionally a staff member would drive a group of the boys to Whiteville to see a movie or take part in some activity and he always asked them to drive by her house, which they did.

Mother had even mentioned to me that perhaps he could stay with her for a while when he got out of Boys Home, but I always discouraged that. As much as she was becoming convinced that he would behave and stay out of trouble, I knew from experience that it probably wouldn't be long before he was sneaking out of the house at night and getting into trouble. I would have loved for him to be there to help her, but I knew that for any extended stay, that probably wouldn't happen. It would have devastated me if the police ever went to her house during the night because he had gotten into trouble. Whiteville is a small town and Mother had her place there as a retired public school supervisor. People knew and respected her. I just couldn't take the chance that she would be put in a position of having to go to the local jail some night to bring him home. It would have subjected her to a life she didn't deserve. So, for those reasons, I didn't encourage that idea.

Jamie did, however, after almost a year, convince her that he was ready to come home. She felt that he was sad and needed the support of his mom and that perhaps he didn't really

35

need to stay two years. And she, in turn, convinced me. In retrospect, I see now that it was a mistake.

Jamie, growing up fast.

Family Time with the Platas

We headed back to the apartment during the afternoon rush hour. I was in a pensive mood and barely aware of the motorcycles, buses, and cars swarming around us during the drive. For a short while, I thought about Jamie and remembered our challenging journey together. We had several good and happy years, too, some of them right here in Cali. I was constantly trying to supplant the memories of the painful experiences with the memories of the fun and loving times. Sometimes it was hard to do and I fought melancholy feelings often as I tried to make sense of our story. Being philosophical didn't help much, but being with loving friends did. It gave me a reprieve from what I was afraid, at times, could be a slow descent into depression. I was happy to see the Chipichape mall in the distance and the entrance to our apartment building.

After a long ride and then quickly freshening up, Marta, Esteban, Sofía, Isa, Isa's boyfriend Pablo and I left for *Obelisco*, the restaurant famous for empanadas. My mood changed considerably as we all piled into Esteban's car and bounced along the city streets on the way to the best empanadas in town.

The hotel *Obelisco* is a small, upscale hotel on a main thoroughfare through the northern part of the city. One of the dining areas is an outdoor space along the Cali River with approximately fifteen tables with umbrellas, across the road from the hotel. Over time, the hotel has become well known for the steaming empanadas prepared in its kitchen, and the tables along the river fill up quickly in the afternoons. Popular among locals, expats, and tourists, most customers are more than willing to wait in line for a table. Empanadas and drinks are the only items served in that area in the afternoon and evening, and waiters navigate the traffic to take and deliver orders from one side of the road to the other. Watching them dodge the cars with trays of food and drinks seems to be a carefully orchestrated spectacle. Occasionally, especially if clients want to cross the road and use the bathrooms in the hotel, one of the waiters will step in the middle of the road, hold up his hand and stop traffic. Remarkably, the traffic stops. I've never heard of anyone being hit by a vehicle there, but honestly, I wouldn't be brave enough to step out in front of traffic like that.

We had our fill of the little hot, fried, meat and/or who-knows-what-else-filled empanadas dipped in chimichurri sauce, made with cilantro, onion, garlic, and vinegar and washed down by beer, juice or cola. The best way to eat them is to take a small bite out of one end, spoon a little sauce inside, and then take a big, fast, bite. A squeeze of a fresh lime adds just the right amount of tartness. The sauce that inevitably runs down your arm just makes the experience more fun. With the bright lights beginning to come on, signaling the coming evening, with the river on one side of us and the noisy traffic on the other, and with Salsa music booming, I recognized again the vibrant, unique energy of Colombia. How could anyone not feel happy in a place like this? I also recognized something special taking place between Isa and Pablo.

We finished up and wiped our faces and mouths one more time before heading out into the night-time traffic. We dropped off Pablo at his parent's house and then Isa told me that she and Pablo had been dating about six years. I found it interesting that they both were college graduates and lived with their parents instead of in their own apartments. That was typical in Colombia and most young people didn't move out until they married. She had a special glow about her that evening and I sensed it wasn't just the empanadas. Hmmmmmmm.

Friday brought another busy day full of gratitude for my friends who arranged events and activities that I had requested. I had checked off yoga classes, areas to walk, Chiquitines, apartments, and today I was going to the beauty parlor, alone, and later, to ride *el Mio*, the new mass transit system in the city. This was especially important since I didn't know if I'd buy a car when-or-if-I finally made the move. Being able to get around the city on my own was extremely important. That evening, I had plans to take them out for my traditional gift to them when I visited – dinner for the whole family in a nice restaurant.

Before going to the beauty parlor, I asked Isa very specifically how to ask the beautician the price of a wash and blow dry. She said, *"Cuanto vale lavarlo y cepillado para mí?"* I wrote it down in my journal that I always keep in my pocketbook when traveling. Apparently there are different prices for long and short hair, so I practiced carefully before leaving the apartment.

The walk from the apartment to the beauty parlor took seven minutes and I went by myself. I think Esteban was watching from the balcony at the apartment. Going out alone didn't seem unusual to me at all and I was happy to be independent again, if only for a short time. As I crossed the street and walked around the gates to Carrefour, the grocery store where the beauty parlor was located, and then across the parking lot, I became acutely aware of a few men on motorcycles parked along the edge of the street. "Why would someone just be sitting on a motorcycle in broad daylight unless they were looking for an easy victim to rob?" I thought. With that thought making my heart race, I straightened up, tried to look confident, and hurried to the building. That familiar feeling of needing to look over my shoulder was still present even though the crime rate in Colombia had gone down since the days when I lived there in the seventies and eighties. The feeling was an ingrained part of my Colombian experience and was important because I knew one still had to be alert and aware of one's surroundings. Becoming too confident could be dangerous and I recalled the incident in Bogotá with the red *ruana* and taxicab when we easily could have been crime victims.

Safely inside and comfortably resting in the hair stylist's chair, I explained what I wanted, we discussed the price, and in less than an hour, my hair was washed, dried and styled. I was more than pleased with how she combed it and mentally checked that off my list. The only other question I had involving the beauty parlor concerned the color process. Maybe it was time to consider letting the gray and silver come through.

From the beauty parlor, I walked next door to the Chipichape mall and strolled around looking at all the people and stores and listening to the sounds. Mostly high-end establishments, they carried the latest fashions and products. A book store was inviting, but I knew I didn't have time to peruse all the magazines and books; however, I was glad to know it was there. A fitness studio on the second floor was full of people working out on machines, but other than that, there were few people milling about. I stopped for a coffee and *pan de bono* and sat down to watch the people. Several were obviously out for their morning walks and looked just like the people doing their laps at Twin Rivers Mall in New Bern on any day of the week. There were a few mothers pushing children in strollers, but because it was early in the day, there were no school age children. There were no young couples, holding hands and strolling. It was comforting to see the security guards who vigilantly guarded the area around the ATM machines.

My trek back to the apartment, which began from a different exit than the one I entered, led me to a side street where I spotted more men on motorcycles. Anxious to get away from that area, I crossed the street just as one of the motorcycles roared to life and headed in my direction. Fortunately, I saw a man in a suit walking on the sidewalk and immediately headed toward him in an attempt to appear with someone and not alone. If the driver of the motorcycle had been headed to me, I'll never know but as soon as I reached the man, the motorcyclist turned off the street and disappeared. My Colombian friends told me that many of these men sitting on motorcycles are security guards, but not all.

When I arrived back at the apartment, Marta had returned from her exercise class and was surprised that I had gone alone to the mall. Esteban assured her that I was fine, but I could tell she was concerned that I had done that. It had to be dealt with, however, because there was no way I could live anywhere and not have the freedom to go out on my own. So I was testing the waters, again, and was convinced that with certain considerations I'd be able to move around comfortably in Cali.

After a specially prepared lunch of the chicken soup *Ajiaco,* one of my favorite Colombian dishes, we all took a siesta. Upon wakening, Esteban and I walked a couple of blocks to catch a ride on *El Mío,* the new transit system in the city. When I found out about this replacement of the public buses, I was thrilled. My memories of the old buses were full of sweaty people crammed into tiny spaces, someone pushing up against me too closely, maybe finding a seat or maybe not. The *Blanco y Negro* buses at that time were more comfortable, but even they were now looking tired and worn out. These new buses were air conditioned, safe, and fast. Esteban told me the crime rate had decreased as a result – tempers didn't flair quite so quickly when people were comfortable. So, *El Mío* was a big positive as I thought more about moving to Cali.

When we got off the bus, after a trip around the city, we were in front of a Home Center store, next door to the Chipichape mall, which was very much like Lowe's and Home Depot in the States.

"Patricia, you can buy anything you need for your apartment here. They have furniture, plants, lamps, kitchen appliances, sheets, everything!" Esteban said. Indeed, it was true. I could probably have furnished my entire apartment here. At that moment, I was struck by the realization that this Cali, this Colombia, would not be the same that I remembered from years ago. In fact, living here would probably be very similar to living in the States. The difference for me, of course, other than the language and an adjustment in the independent manner in which I was accustomed to living, would be my Colombian families, and the majestic Andes – two strong ties.

Back at the apartment, there was an air of excitement as we all dressed and prepared for our dinner out. Esteban opened a bottle of wine and poured glasses for the adults, which we sipped while freshening up and changing clothes. The beat of Salsa music filled the apartment and we danced around each other while getting ready.

"Patricia, Isa's boyfriend Pablo is going with us tonight, but he will pay his own way. We do not expect you to pay for his dinner," Esteban said. We had been through this kind of thing before so I didn't say much when he said that, but I knew I would offer to pay for Pablo's dinner when the check came. Gladly.

There was a lot of chattering while we dressed and I could hear them talking about Colombia's soccer team, which had not had a good season. When I asked about it, someone said, "It's because they drink too much. They're drunk most of the time." There were lots of laughs, but I felt that the comment was nothing more than an attempt to not take their poor performance that season too seriously.

In the past, I had always let Esteban and Marta choose the restaurant where I would treat them. Tonight we were going to a fashionable and popular new restaurant called *Platillos Voladores* (roughly translated, Flying Dishes) on 9th Avenue in the Granada neighborhood. Voted "Best in Cali" three years in a row, the restaurant offered a fusion style menu with beef, chicken, and seafood dishes, served in a cozy, soft-lit ambience with open spaces and soft breezes. When we arrived, I noticed the handsome and husky men standing around and I mentioned something to Marta about it. She explained that they were security. I was not unaccustomed to having security nearby, but these were a different type and their appearance was very non-threatening - to us, anyway. In fact, they were very attractive. Attentive waiters hovered close by and we all relaxed and enjoyed our meal. Pablo, Isa's boyfriend, was very polite, as he had been on the night we ate *empanadas*, but shy with me. I chose a seafood dish and was served a bountiful amount that was delectable and prepared with skill. Most everybody else opted for beef and seemed to be pleased with their choices. After a long and satisfying meal, I paid the bill and noted that for the first time in all the restaurants I had visited in Colombia, the charges seemed excessive. I probably wouldn't be coming to this restaurant on a regular basis, but the expense for this one night was worth every penny. We lingered as long as we could and enjoyed the soft music and cool breezes. Finally, we headed outside and climbed in the cars. Security hovered around us until all of the car doors were closed and locked and we were pulling out into traffic.

This was the last night I would spend with Esteban and his family until he took me to the airport a few days later. They were attending a wedding out of town and I would spend time with Ximena and her family before heading back home.

The author with the Plata family, eating empanadas at the restaurant *Obelisco*.

CHIMICHURRI

There are many variations on this sauce, not only in South and Latin America, but in Colombia itself. The following recipe was given to me by my friend Ximena and is one that is easy to make with ingredients found in the United States. Other variations include chopped tomato and/or chiles. I serve it as a condiment with chicken soup (my own interpretation of Ajiaco), as well as with meats and as a topping for sandwiches.

Chop finely:

Green onions

Cilantro

Garlic

Blend together (in the quantity you desire) with white vinegar and a little water. Keeps several days in the refrigerator.

Chapter Four

On the Road with the Francos, 2010

Mosquito Nets and Lizards

Early the next morning, a little sleepy from the celebration the previous night, Isa and I left the apartment and drove to the south side of the city where we met Ximena. I moved my suitcase from Isa's car to Ximena's car and then went inside the grocery store to use the ATM machine. Ximena was always cautious and protective of me and hesitated when I told her I needed to get some pesos. I don't think she had ever used an ATM machine herself and was concerned about the security.

"Why don't you wait until we see Rafael? He can go with you," she said. There were times that I felt shackled when I was with Ximena and I always tried hard not to bristle when the apron strings were tightened. In this case, I trusted my instincts and told her I'd be OK. I entered the grocery store and used the machine without incidence while she kept a watchful eye.

With suitcases packed and pesos in tow, we started off on the one hour trip to Jamundi, where Ximena and Rafael were baby-sitting their granddaughter, Salomé. Rafael had driven down earlier in the morning and was with Salomé now. Her parents, Margarita and Ricardo, were attending a wedding in Medellin and would be gone overnight. They promised to return to Cali late in the afternoon on Monday to pick up

Salomé. I had never been to Jamundi, but I remembered hearing my former students at Colegio Bolívar talk about it. We passed the school on the way out of town and I remembered them saying that Jamundi was extremely hot – with no breezes and no river. It had, however, become a popular, gated community for well-to-do, professional residents, and the people who lived there went to clubs to swim and cool off. Most of the houses had pools. There was a small town with a few stores and shops and a small number of people lived and worked in the area.

The sun was especially hot that morning, and Ximena apologized for the broken air-conditioner in the car. I was dressed in lightweight cotton, hair was in a ponytail, and the windows were rolled down. I was fine. We sped by the sugarcane fields, unable to talk because of the noise, and covered our noses and laughed when the stench from animal waste overwhelmed us. And dust! There was always dust from road projects or the fields. Soon we rolled into town where our plan was to pick up the maid, and came upon a circular park in the middle of the road. I thought, briefly, of the courthouse in my hometown of Whiteville and the many times I rode around it with friends. Learning how to navigate the circle traffic was a rite of passage for teenagers at that time. As we headed into the circle, a wagon, pulled by four horses, suddenly came barreling into the intersection. There was one driver, and three men sat on a bench behind him. They were sitting upright, with cowboy hats on, probably hanging on for dear life. The driver was cracking the reins and the horses were galloping full speed ahead. As the wagon entered the circle, it tilted on two wheels, righted itself and never lost a beat. As quickly as it appeared, it just as quickly exited the circle and went off in another direction. Ximena had to stop the car to let them pass and we both sat there for a minute staring at all the dust and the commotion the runaway wagon had caused. I regretted not having my camera handy.

We eased back into traffic, shaking our heads and laughing, and set off to find the house where the maid lived. Ximena stopped a few times to get directions and she soon found the house where the maid was waiting for us. After picking her up, we drove to the house which Margarita and Ricardo were renting and pulled into the driveway. It was a lovely house, Spanish style, with mature, lush landscaping.

Inside, there was very little furniture, but they had what they needed. With an open courtyard in the center of the house, there was plenty of shade and the temperature was comfortable. I spotted a hammock and beautiful tile floors and soon saw Rafael and Salomé. I had not seen Rafael on the trip the year before which meant I hadn't seen him since 1986. He had had health issues, but all accounts indicated he was doing well and progressing. Ximena was concerned about him, but assured me that being a grandfather was bringing him much joy.

Ximena and I brought our bags in and then quickly got back in the car with Rafael and Salomé. We needed groceries and left for the mall where we had a lunch of chicken sandwiches and lemonade. Ximena bought a few things in the grocery store and Rafael and I walked around and looked at the fruits and vegetables. It was a fast trip, but Salomé had a dancing class and we needed to get her there on time.

Once back at the house, we took a few minutes to put up the groceries and get settled in before walking a couple of blocks to the clubhouse where the class was held. While Salomé and her friends practiced the Salsa, Ximena and I stood on the sidelines and danced along to the music. Rafael went to the pool for a quick swim and then we walked back to the house. Somehow, in the midst of all this activity, we managed to rest a little before getting ready for the trip back to Cali and the class reunion at Colegio Bolívar.

For many years the school held a reunion in June for all former students, teachers and friends. I was looking forward to going and perhaps seeing former students and colleagues. Carolina Chavez, the alumni director, and I had been in touch and she assured me that I was welcome to bring someone with me. Although I'm sure Ximena was tired and would have preferred to stay home and relax, she insisted on going with me while Rafael babysat Salomé.

We left the house around 4 p.m. and arrived on campus by 5. Not many people had arrived at that time, but the colorful and festive decorations were up in the open-air gym and food vendors were setting up their carts. Musicians were checking their equipment and I was thinking that I should have brought ear plugs with me. I could smell the empanadas and hoped we'd be able to try some, as well as some of the other food. Carolina was busy checking on details and people were beginning to mill around. Soon there would be dancing and partying big time. There would be greetings and hugs and picture-taking. Whether or not any of my former students would be there, I couldn't say. As it turned out, I didn't run into any of them, but the objective of attending a reunion was met and at 6:30, after a plateful of empanadas, Ximena and I decided to return to Jamundi.

By 7:30, we were back at Margarita's house having a glass of wine relaxing in the courtyard. Rafael and I talked for a long time while Ximena tried to get Salomé to bed. By 10:30, after a long day, we were getting ready to turn in. My room was on the ground floor with several large arched windows which had shutters, and lightweight, thin curtains. Outside the open windows I could see, and nearly touch, orange and mandarin trees, wild flowers, and a huge palm tree. As was typical in Colombia, there were no screens on the windows. Rafael helped me arrange the mosquito net around my bed and I closed the windows. During the day, the net was rolled to the ceiling and then lowered at night. There was an opening in the net where one could enter and it was important to close it tightly after getting in bed. After wrestling with the net I finally slept.

The next morning, I awoke early and walked to the adjoining bathroom and took a shower. The cold water felt crisp and I quickly noticed a couple of ferocious mosquito bites that had apparently happened during the night, in spite of the net. After getting dressed, I returned to the bedroom and walked to the windows to pull the curtains back and open the shutters.

Perched on the inside of the window, and also on the curtain, were a few lizards. They didn't seem to be alarmed by the sudden movement and I was just grateful they were there and not in my bed. I had run into lizards in Colombia before and was told they were welcome because they ate mosquitos. Apparently, the mosquitos were considered more of a threat than the lizards. Birds were waking up and announcing their arrival in what had transformed itself into an early morning paradise. I quickly rolled up the mosquito net and went to the kitchen for breakfast. Ximena was cutting up papaya and mangos and soon we were enjoying the fruit, toast, orange juice and coffee.

We packed up quickly after breakfast and by 9 o'clock, Ximena, Rafael, Salomé and I were back on the road headed to Cali. Saturday night babysitting services done! Rafael dropped his car off at the apartment in Cali and soon we were all in Ximena's car headed to Lake Calima where the clouds, at certain times of the day, seemed to gently fold themselves around the mountains. They reminded me of well-washed muslin fabric draped like full skirts over a chair. I was looking forward to that view again.

Ximena and Salomé, reading *The Twelve Days of Christmas in North Carolina.*

Lake Calima Revisited

The heat in the car with no air conditioning was nearly unbearable, but with Rafael now driving for the two hour trip to Lake Calima, and with the windows rolled down, we were zipping along and adjusting to the temperature. The cooler air could always be felt at a certain point in the trip and someone always mentioned it.

"Patricia," said Rafael, "can you feel the change in temperature? Take a deep breath and you can almost smell the lake."

It was true and I immediately felt relief as we drew closer and closer to the lake. I didn't think we'd be going swimming in the lake today, but there was a chance we'd get in María Isabel's Jacuzzi and the anticipation of that was heavenly.

"Yes! I'm feeling better already, Mr. Andretti," I shouted. Calling Rafael by some Italian race car driver's name had become an inside joke in the many years I had been riding with him. I always accused him of thinking he was a famous European Grand Prix driver. He didn't seem to mind and Ximena thought it was funny. She always insisted that I ride in the front seat, and as a result, I couldn't avoid watching the way he drove. He was fearless! And she didn't have to watch too closely from the back seat.

Before going to *La Casa Azul*, Maria Isabel's house, we stopped in the little town of Darien to have lunch. Just a few miles from the lake, Darien is a lovely quaint pueblo with a central park surrounded by a church, small stores and eating establishments. Early in the evening, people gather in the park to visit with friends and enjoy the cool temperatures. There is usually always live music, and children scamper around with their friends and family. Young girls lock arms and stroll together, singing songs and doing steps their ancestors probably did. On Tuesdays, artisans come to town and set up their wares on the streets. I've been to the market many times and have always come away with something beautiful and unique – usually something handmade like jewelry.

"This is it," Ximena said, as we slowly drove through the streets, avoiding the potholes when possible. "This is the new restaurant that's supposed to be so good." She pointed to a small open air establishment which was very typical of all the others. Rafael soon found a parking space, right on the street, and we rolled up the windows and locked the doors. The roads in these small towns were often in bad shape and, as a result, it was necessary to jump over holes and broken pavement - widow makers, as they were called - as we got out of the car. Several tables and chairs, which could have come straight from a 1950s kitchen in the States, filled the space, with a small counter and cash register tucked away in a corner. Each table had salt and pepper shakers, napkins, and bottled sauces. Advertisements for chicken and beef dishes were displayed on the walls. There was a huge Pepsi poster which made me think immediately of New Bern, where I lived, and where Pepsi was created back in the late 1890s. That was the first time I had seen a Pepsi advertisement in Colombia. The most popular soft drink from the States here was Coke. With no walls around the front of the restaurant, it was impossible to keep the flies out, so they, along with a dog or two, were a part of the clientele.

We ordered either beef or chicken and soon were served the first course which was always soup. The soup was usually enough for me but when an order for lunch was placed, it included the entire meal. So I enjoyed a small amount of the soup and saved room for the other dishes. My chicken dish was one half a chicken, moist and roasted to a golden brown, served with potatoes, salad and an *arepa*, similar to a roll but made with corn meal. The drink was Pepsi, but I stuck with the bottled water I carried in my pocketbook. I'm ordinarily a slow eater, and that day was no different. However, by the time I had eaten all I could, which was only a small portion of the food,

Ximena and Rafael had finished and were waiting for dessert, a sweet cake.

It was all delicious, everything was clean and the service was attentive. I remembered well how easily and quickly I had gained weight when I lived in Colombia the first time, in 1975. I hoped I was beyond that now, but there's no doubt the food in Colombia could be addictive. I was never sure if it was due to travelers' hunger or the food itself. I had noticed, too, that people no longer clapped their hands when they wanted their bill as I had seen them do in years past. That custom had always seemed somewhat disrespectful and demeaning, so I was happy to find out that it was no longer acceptable.

Our bill was approximately four dollars each.

Before getting back in the car for the short trip to the lake, we took a leisurely stroll around the park. I noticed that a few of the stores had *ruanas,* the Colombian version of the poncho and serape, hanging on racks in their doorways. The nights were cool here and many people still wore them. This symbol of Colombia was seared in my mind from the days in Bogotá and I missed seeing people wear them now. During my recent trips to Bogotá, I rarely saw people wearing *ruanas.* If I did, it was usually older men, in a time-honored tradition, still protecting themselves from the wind and cold rain with the perfectly appropriate item of clothing. Their clothes were modern now and people wore down jackets and blazers. My own two *ruanas,* however, were safely tucked away in my closet at home and would always be there. I had jokingly told my family in the States that perhaps they should drape my beautiful red *ruana* over my coffin or place it on a table under the urn with my ashes when I died. Maybe I really wasn't joking. After a good twenty-minute walk, we returned to the car and were ready to finally go to the lake.

María Isabel, Ximena and Rafael's older daughter, was waiting for us at her house, *La Casa Azul,* the blue house, on the banks of Lake Calima. Her husband, Dr. Muñoz, known as "Mellizo" (twin) and their two sons, Juan Miguel and José

Tomás, along with José Tomás' friend, were waiting for us. They helped us unpack the car and then left to go boating in the lake. We had a short siesta before enjoying coffee and cookies. These little siestas were usually short and always injected us with a much needed dose of energy. Afterwards we relaxed and talked and sat in the Jacuzzi. Eventually, the boys returned and activity around the house picked up. They jumped on the in-ground trampoline and played with the dogs in the fenced-in yard. The adults played cards outside on a table set up beside the Jacuzzi. There was an outdoor shower made with beautiful, smooth, river rocks and a sauna for anyone interested. A small, tiled bathroom was also available close to the shower. The bougainvillea was lush and the orange trees provided plenty of shade. While the others were playing cards or chasing the dogs, I sat outdoors in a comfortable chair and used a small table to write and make notes. The sun, the shade, the crisp air, the view of the water, all inspired me here. I loved this quiet time when I was visiting with my friends and I always appreciated the fact that no one expected me to do anything else. They knew I was writing a book and that jotting down facts was a part of it.

Esmeralda, the maid, was stirring up a beef mixture for tacos, (not a Colombian dish), and I could smell onions and unknown seasonings. Soon, she brought us wine and crackers and before dark, we all sat down – eight of us - at the long table and enjoyed a satisfying meal. Esmeralda's daughter, Sara Ximena, four years old at the time, lived at the house with her mother and helped her serve the table. She was an adorable little girl and a very fortunate one, also. The two of them stayed in a two-room apartment in the basement, had a TV, nice bathroom, comfortable furnishings, and took care of the house when the Muñoz family was there and when they were not. Not many domestic helpers in Colombia had such accommodating employers, and there were plans for Sara Ximena to attend the local school when she was the right age.

While we were eating, one of the two family dogs roamed around in the living room. The other one walked around outside and we could see him through the long glass windows. He carried a huge banana leaf in his mouth and rarely ever let it go. The boys said he had always done that. The inside dog was old and deaf, and, like dogs who live to be a certain age, he would lose bladder control at any time. And, so, right there in the dining room where we were eating that lovely meal, it happened. Mellizo and María Isabel were horrified and they and Esmeralda quickly cleaned up the mess. They apologized and took the dog out, but for them, it spoiled the evening. The rest of us tried to ease their concerns, but there was not much we could do. Poor doggie.

That night was a symphony of musical beds. I was to sleep in the bedroom with José Tomás and his friend, but soon after we all turned in, the friend got sick and threw up in his bed. María Isabel came in, and took him to a bed in another room. We both cleaned up the bed and floor. José Tomás wanted to be with his friend so María Isabel and Mellizo moved to the bedroom in the guest cottage and the boys stayed in their room. I had seen more lizards around the windows, and even though I now had the room to myself, I spent a restless night.

Activity resumed early the next morning when Alexandra, Mellizo's twin sister, and her son arrived to spend the day with us. Exuberant and friendly, Alexandra didn't look much like Mellizo, but she was glamorous, spoke good English and seemed happy to see all of us. Her teenage son was handsome and eager to practice his English.

After a big breakfast of fresh orange juice, papaya, toast, pancakes, eggs and coffee made in the *calcetin* – the sock apparatus which I had discovered in Bogotá many years ago - María Isabel, Alexandra and I went for a walk.

Immediately behind the house there were a couple of barns and a couple of cows being tended by a worker who was mending a fence. María Isabel knew him (in fact, this was a part of their property) and stopped to chat for a few minutes. We continued up the hill where we could now see other impressive looking houses – some in a state of disrepair. It appeared that most of them were empty and María Isabel told us that many had been owned by members of the Mafioso. When that crime-ridden segment of the local population had been brought under control, many of the houses were abandoned. But not all. As we approached one house down a narrow dirt road, we could hear music blaring but did not see any signs of activity.

"Often when owners are away they use the loud music as a guise to keep potential thieves away. It doesn't always work, but there is usually always someone, such as a maid, living in the house when the owners are away, music or not," María Isabel explained. I admired the beautiful tile in the courtyards and pools and thought about the potential of the property.

Another house had a hand-painted "for sale" sign in the front yard. While we were walking around this area, we occasionally saw docile horses or cows on the side of the road. They were roped to trees or fences and kept the vegetation under control. I always thought of them as Colombian lawnmowers.

About the same time that I was getting ready to ask if the Mafioso were still in this area, we saw a car inching its way down the bumpy road. I remembered that Pablo Escobar, the notorious, now deceased, drug lord, had lived and played nearby. Four motorcycles were slowly escorting an expensive-looking vehicle with tinted windows. We stepped aside to avoid being covered in dust and watched as the entourage continued up the hill. Soon they were out of sight and I immediately asked María Isabel if she knew who was in the car.

"It could be an important government official or a member of the Mafioso," she said. "We see cars like this occasionally in this area, but at this time, we are not worried. We feel that we are well protected and there are always guards watching our property." I still admired my Colombian friends for being willing to co-exist with threats from the presence of the drug culture.

By this time, the heat from the rising sun was intensifying and we decided to return to the house. Covered in dust, we all showered before a short rest and preparation for the early afternoon meal.

In time, Esmeralda lit the fire for the gas grill. While we all relaxed and enjoyed a leisurely afternoon outside, Alexandra and I started talking about food. She enjoyed cooking and used herbs in much the same way that I did. Other than cilantro, I had not found fresh herbs used frequently here in Colombia, but I felt sure that I had just not been in the right kitchens. I especially enjoyed thyme, basil, marjoram, and tarragon and grew them in my own garden. With so many prepared foods now available in the markets here, I was afraid fresh herbs were being used less and less in local kitchens. That certainly happened in the States at one time, but there was a growing segment of people there who were now focused on returning to using fresh herbs, myself included. Alexandra assured me that herbs were still being used, but that the canned soups and sauces found in the markets now saved a lot of time for the many women who worked outside the home. It all sounded so familiar. So Alexandra shared a few recipes with me that I felt I'd be able to adapt to my own preferences, using ingredients available in the States. One reason I was so happy to get these recipes was that now I could prove that Colombian food was not all about *arepas, empanadas, maranitas* and other similar dishes – tasty food, for sure, but all fried in hot oil.

Before having a chance to write down recipes, the bell sounded that signified our meal was ready. No one needed a bell to remind us of that, since the aroma from the grill had already put us on alert. Mellizo had joined in the activity at the cooking station and was shuffling food around and shouting orders. There were pieces of pork, chicken, beef and hot dogs sizzling together. Slices of eggplant topped with tomato and cheese vied for space. I couldn't tell if spices and/or herbs had been used, but it all smelled delicious – and charred. Esmeralda brought out a salad of lettuce, tomato, mushrooms and cheese and placed it on the table. We each then filled our plates with the food from the grill and passed around the salad as we prepared to enjoy this bountiful meal. Large pitchers of lemonade and papaya juice were on the table. Ordinarily there would have been wine and/or beer also, but we were planning to drive back to the city later in the afternoon and the drivers were conscientious about not mixing alcohol and gasoline. We ate and talked and laughed and listened to some Colombian country music.

We wrapped up the meal with *tinto*, small cups of strong coffee, and then prepared for our afternoon siestas. The men and boys stretched out on sofas and chairs and watched a soccer match on TV while the women helped in the kitchen. Esmeralda had everything under control so we soon took our own siestas in the bedrooms. This had been a typical Colombian holiday afternoon and not unlike what many families in the States did after a big meal – except for the extra help in the kitchen.

By 4 p.m. we were packed and ready to return to Cali. There was still a lot to do this afternoon so no one tarried. We arrived at Ximena and Rafael's apartment a little after 6 p.m. where Margarita and Ricardo were waiting to pick up Salomé. Once they were gone, Ximena and Rafael and I sat down to watch the evening news on TV.

We were waiting for Esteban to come pick me up and take me back to his apartment. The news concerned four Colombian men, kidnapped twelve years earlier by FARC, who had just been released. President Uribe spoke to the citizens as he honored these brave and courageous men who were gathered in a room with the President, aides, news people and family members. I couldn't understand all of the Spanish, but I had no doubt that the men were being recognized for their contributions to the peace effort. Each man, showing signs of exhaustion and deprivation, spoke briefly, struggling to be strong.

"This is a very emotional time for Colombians," Rafael said, with a great sense of gravity. Just then the doorbell rang and Esteban arrived. I was sorry we didn't have time to talk more, but it was time to go. I said my goodbyes to Rafael and Ximena and they sent me off with wishes for a safe trip and a quick return to Colombia.

We were up early the next morning for the trip to the airport. On the way there, as dawn was breaking over the mountains, Esteban said, "Patricia, what are you thinking?"

"Right now, my head is spinning. I'm thinking about finishing my book and selling my house. When that happens, then I'll make plans to return," I said.

"Don't forget, we're your Colombian family and you will always have a room here. We love you."

With that, Esteban took the airport exit and I was soon on my way home, back to New Bern, with a lot to think about.

A view of Lake Calima, from the *finca* of Esteban Plata.

Jamie – Serious Incarcerations

At the age of twelve, when Jamie returned from Boys Home, he was still under the psychiatric care of a physician in Wilmington. After a few months, I located someone in New Bern to work with him, and he appeared to be on stable ground. For a while I was encouraged by his progress, but soon after school started I began receiving calls from his teachers that he was being disrespectful and disruptive in the classroom. His doctor adjusted his medication a number of times, and Jamie skidded on an emotional roller coaster for several months. He was either hyper and unmanageable or depressed and withdrawn.

This all came to a head one day when the guidance counselor at my school came to my classroom and told me that I needed to go to the hospital. Jamie had taken an overdose of aspirin before catching the bus for school, and then called his guidance counselor. She called 911 and they transported him to the hospital. By the time I got there, he was in the emergency room receiving treatment. The nurses assured me that physically, he would be okay. It appeared that the overdose, as is often the case, was a plea for help. I sat by his bed, holding his hand, trying to let him know that I loved and cared about him very much. He didn't talk, but he did respond by squeezing my hand often. As I tried to fathom what he was thinking, recurring images kept appearing in my mind of the carefree, joyful little boy so full of promise.

He was sent to Cherry Hospital in Goldsboro for three weeks to the adolescent psychiatric unit where I was allowed to visit twice during the week and Sunday afternoons. I would leave school after work and drive the hour and a half to spend thirty minutes with him, return, and also go on Sundays. I was always encouraged when I saw him on these trips because he was sweet, calm, and responsive with me. He was being treated for depression which was always experimental.

When he left the hospital, his team at Cherry recommended that he attend a residential program here in New Bern until his doctors felt he was ready to reintegrate in the public schools. I found a new doctor to treat him, and for a while, Jamie responded positively to her treatment. She acknowledged that many of his difficulties could be explained by his social background (his adoption from Colombia at the age of seven) and by the history of recurring episodes of depression. Over a year's time, she noted that "he has shown marked improvement in his affect and mood and behaviors since being started on Wellbutrin. He is showing an increased sense of responsibility both at home and in school and, when last seen on 12/7/93, was working out details with his mother for beginning a job and buying a car. Since I was able to observe the patient's behavior, both a full year ago and at present, I can unequivocally say that the patient has shown a remarkable change of attitude and his interest and motivation have improved tenfold." Nothing could have given me more hope than this report.

We moved from the cramped condo in Riverbend to a more spacious house in Trent Woods. With more space, inside and out, we both enjoyed working in the garden and being closer to his activities at school and the YMCA. When mother came to visit, we all had our own bedrooms and Jamie was happy to help her cook, clean, or do whatever she asked him to do. The new house was a positive step for us.

During the next several years, however, as he was moving through his teens, he would often stop taking his medication without telling me. He became defiant and started experimenting with drugs. He dropped out of the day school program and registered for night school which allowed him to work during the day. His schedule varied, depending on his job, but he was still living at home. It was during this time that he seemed to spiral downward rapidly. I never knew to what extent he was involved in buying and selling drugs, but

I was aware that his behavior was deteriorating. He could go from being a sweet, gentle, kind boy who worked hard and held responsible jobs, to a stranger who once punched a hole in the living room wall because I wouldn't let him have one of my suitcases when he wanted to move out. On another occasion, he walked down the hall in our house with a butcher knife in his hand and headed to my room. When I confronted him and sensed immediately a dangerous situation, I said calmly, "Jamie, you know you aren't supposed to bring dishes and food to the bedrooms." With that he stopped, turned around, and went back into the kitchen. After an incident when he was charged with possession of marijuana and taken to the city jail, I left home and drove downtown to pick him up. It was after midnight on a school night and it was the start of a pattern that repeated itself many times.

It was one of my first trips to pick him up, and I was stunned by the seriousness of the situation and crushed by his demeanor. This particular time, he was composed and didn't appear to be under the influence of drugs or alcohol. The straight-back chair he sat in appeared to prop him up, giving support, and exposing him at the same time. When he looked at me, I felt an overwhelming aura of defeat and sadness about him that seemed to saturate every pore in his body and which also slammed against my psyche with the force of a baseball bat. He was stone cold sober that night, and for some reason, had chosen to be involved in an illegal drug activity. Was it money? Peer pressure? When my head stopped spinning, I immediately slipped back into my maternal mode. This was the boy who could marvel at the beauty of a sunrise on the beach and bring home an abandoned kitten he found outside a restaurant where he worked. A gentle soul existed among the demons.

After that first incident, he moved out of the house and into a trailer with people I didn't know. He moved to the beach and got in trouble there as well. It wasn't long before he was sent to correctional institutions and all I could do was visit him on weekends.

These turbulent years had deteriorated into periods of real instability and legal maneuverings. Each release from incarceration would be followed by a period of hope that this was the last time he would commit felonious acts. But it never seemed to stop.

One morning, I opened the local newspaper and saw this article: "The thefts, all from safes inside the building, netted him nearly $16,000. Many checks were found but the money is still missing." When I saw this, with his name on the headline, his behavior a few days earlier made sense. He had stopped by the house one morning before this crime was committed. I was working in the garden in the front yard and wasn't surprised at all to see him riding someone's bike and coming to a stop about ten feet from where I was standing. He had done that before, just appearing out of nowhere, and now he was back, I was sure, to try one more time to talk me into lending him one hundred dollars. His share of the rent was due on Monday.

He had called a few days earlier to ask the favor and I had told him that I didn't have any extra money. Saying no to him was sometimes hard to do, especially when I knew it might mean he'd be sleeping on the streets if he couldn't come up with his share of the rent – but I had reached the point that I felt I had no choice. So, today's visit was to try again. He didn't say that was why he was there and I knew he wouldn't.

After a while he said he wanted to clean out his car, which was parked under a shed in the backyard, and wanted to know if he could use the vacuum cleaner. This sudden interest in cleaning out a car that had a broken window, no license tag, and more garbage than I had in the kitchen trash can caught me by surprise. He had lost his driver's license and wouldn't be able to get a new one for several months. The agreement was that the car would stay at my house until his debts were paid, and then, if he could get his license and pay the insurance, he would be free to take the car. It wasn't long before he told me he was trying to sell the car and wanted to clean it up before a prospective buyer came to look at it. So that was it. He wanted to sell the car to get the money he needed for the rent. I let him use the vacuum cleaner and thought that selling the car was probably a good idea.

Several days later, after the encounter in the front yard, he called the police from a motel room and confessed to having broken into four restaurants and stolen cash and checks in the amount of $16,000. I later found out, after the police came and searched the house, that he had hidden approximately $9,000 in checks in the attic while I was at school one day. He spent the remainder on clothes, food, entertainment, and the rent.

He was arrested immediately and taken to the county jail while awaiting arraignment.

Inmates whose last names began with "W" were allowed visitors on Sunday afternoons from two o'clock until five o'clock. On the first Sunday after Jamie turned himself in to the authorities, I was so full of anger that I didn't consider going to the jail.

The following week I was anxious, but ready to see my son. Ordinarily, visitors check in and wait to be called on a first-come, first-serve basis. That day, however, I was called in immediately and taken to a holding cell where Jamie had been placed under a suicide watch. I was told that he had not eaten for three days and would be taken to the hospital if he didn't eat something by that night. I was encouraged to talk to him, but was reminded that I couldn't touch him. No hugging, patting on the back or getting too close. A guard stood close by.

When I walked in the cell, he was lying on his cot, facing the wall. I stood at the door and gently and quietly told him how much we all loved him and were going to do everything we could to help him. He never looked at me. Later that night, I received a call from the jail saying he drank some juice.

The next Sunday, he wouldn't see me at all. The few times I eventually saw him, he was despondent and withdrawn, just as he had been with his attorney, the investigator, and our neighbor who is a minister. He slumped over the table and rarely looked at me when I was there. When I did get a response, it was nothing more than a yes or no.

His attorney stayed in touch with me and told me he would recommend that Jamie be evaluated at Dorothea Dix Hospital because he didn't think he could participate in his own defense. It had been my feeling all along that this needed to be done before any more attempts to rehabilitate him could take place, and I was greatly relieved when the judge approved the recommendation.

While Jamie remained in the local jail, I continued to visit him on Sundays. On the days he agreed to see me, I saw very little change. When he finally did look at me, he had such a terrified expression on his face that my stomach lurched and any composure I might have had withered and died.

We didn't make much progress, or change our routine until a later visit. One day he walked in the visiting booth with a little bounce in his step and the tiniest bit of a grin. Could this be the same Jamie I had worried about so desperately for the last few weeks? At that moment, I didn't care that he had broken the law so many times. I was never going to give up on him. All I was concerned about was that he was showing signs of the spirited person he once was. Maybe now there was something that I, or somebody, could do to help him. He seemed genuinely happy to see me.

Mom: Hi, Jamie. How's it going, sweetheart?

Jamie: Pretty good. I thought you were going to Raleigh today.

Mom: Well, I just got back and I wanted to see you.

Jamie: But you've already been here four times today.

Mom: Hmm? I did come to see you last week but this is the first time today.

Jamie: This is the first day of my sentence and I'll be out soon.

Mom: Have you talked to your attorney, Mr. Weaver, this week? Did he come by to see you?

Looking at the wall, there was a nod.

Mom: What did you talk about?

Jamie: God.

Mom: Are you sure that was your attorney or was it our neighbor, Reverend Singleton?

Jamie: It was the preacher.

Mom: Good. I'm glad he came to see you. He's very concerned about you and hopes his visits will help you. Have you talked to Mr. Weaver?

Jamie: I don't have a lawyer. When I turned myself in they placed me under a $25,000 bond but they didn't arrest me. So I don't need a lawyer.

Mom: Has anyone talked to you about going to the hospital for the tests? You remember our talking about it, don't you? It's much nicer than this place and you'll have lots of activities and things to do.

Jamie: Why did you say I'm going to the hospital?

Mom: It's not because you're sick, honey. It's because they'd like to get to know you better so they can help you.

Jamie: Well, I'm serving my sentence now.

Mom: Have you been to court yet?

No answer, just a questioning look.

Mom: You know, you'll have to go to court first and then the judge will tell you what your sentence will be.

This time it was just a blank stare and I struggled to make some sense out of his responses. Coming close to panicking and going into shock myself, I managed to find a scrap of paper to jot down a few notes. Somehow I had to let someone know what he was saying and I knew the notes would help me remember. Silence followed until I changed the conversation.

Our next encounter, a few days later, continued in the same vein.

Mom: You're looking better today, Jamie. Are you eating your meals now?

Jamie: Yeah. Today I had 130 trays.

Mom: 130 trays?

Jamie: Yeah.

Mom: What kind of food did they bring you? The same thing on all the trays?

Jamie: No.

Mom: Well, you really are looking a lot better. I hope you'll eat everything they bring you. Are you exercising any?

Jamie: I did some pushups.

Mom: Good. Are you in the cell by yourself?

Jamie: It's not my room. I'm just borrowing it.

Mom: Do you get to see the other inmates? Do you know any of them?

Jamie: Yep, I've got a new nickname: "freak."

Mom: They call you "freak?"

Jamie: I drank some piss today.

Mom: You drank some what today?

Jamie: Piss.

Mom: Honey, I'm having a hard time hearing you through this screen. What did you say you drank? Tell me again.

Jamie: Piss

Mom: Okay. Ask someone for water if you get thirsty. They'll get some for you.

Jamie: This has been a long day.

Mom: What have you done? Did you try some of the puzzles I brought you?

Jamie: 130 trays. I am FULL.

And so the conversation continued for about ten more minutes. With probing he rambled, talking about the long day, his nickname, 130 trays, and drinking piss. When the guard came to tell us our time was up, Jamie got up and walked out of the room without saying anything. As I watched him leave, I also watched the world he once knew disappear and I struggled to hold on to the last glimmer of hope for him.

It wasn't long before he was taken to Dorothea Dix Hospital for evaluation and from there, at the young age of 19, sent to Maury Correctional Institution for two and a half years. During the time he was away I, at times, felt like I hated him and at times felt extreme remorse for not doing a better job of parenting. I blamed myself for a lot of his problems, but I never allowed myself to wallow in self-pity because I knew, deep down, that I had done the very best I could.

Going to work was a blessing and at times a curse. A blessing because it forced me to think about other things and a curse because there were students at school who knew Jamie and they could, at times, be cruel. There were constant reminders: not only the students themselves, but his former teachers, who were supportive and non-judgmental, and colleagues who had watched his downfall unfold. One teacher, in particular, had noticed one morning when she came to work a few years earlier that the license plate on my car was missing. It was necessary for me to leave school, and she volunteered to keep my class while I went home and discovered that Jamie had removed it from my car and put it on his car. The guidance counselor at school had been one of the first to arrive at the hospital after he took an overdose of aspirin. These incidents were common and I received a lot of support from my friends in the workplace.

I cleaned out his room where, even though he had moved out a few times before, a lot of his things were still stored, and I nearly threw out all of the mementos from Colombia. Something held me back from discarding his artwork and report cards from Colegio Bolívar. The beautiful handmade card from my colleagues there, with congratulatory wishes when his adoption finally came through, and the birthday and Christmas cards he had made for me when he was much younger, eventually found their way to a storage box for safekeeping and my anger slowly subsided.

In time, he wrote me letters from prison that were philosophical in nature and usually full of remorse. He wrote poignant poetry. I'm sure that getting off drugs helped clear his mind and he actually seemed to mature. He was in his early twenties now. As soon as he was allowed to have visitors, I started making the hour and half trip from New Bern to Maury on Sundays, and occasionally Mother went with me. We sat in a big open dining room and had snacks and soft drinks, bought on the grounds, while we, and other inmates and their families, talked. He was shy, and sweet, and seemed genuinely happy to see me. When possible, we took a few pictures and when I look at those pictures now I see a very sad mother. Jamie had gained weight, and at six foot three, he was a big man. The work of the on-site barber left something to be desired, but at least he had lost that wild, manic, demeanor he had during his most difficult times. I could actually imagine him groomed and dressed in something other than prison garb. While he was incarcerated, he took advantage of the GED program and was proud of finally earning his high school degree which would enable him to later receive further training at a community college or vocational school.

Near the end of his incarceration, I started receiving mail from the prison social workers with updates and recommendations for him once he was released. Jamie and I had talked about his future plans and had both agreed that he should go to some town other than New Bern, where there were still many reminders of the past. We both agreed that he needed a fresh start. The social worker felt that even though she didn't think that returning to New Bern would be a good idea, she did suggest he try some place familiar to him. With that suggestion in mind, we started thinking about Wilmington, which was close to Whiteville and also where some of his cousins lived. He was familiar with the area. It was less than two hours from New Bern and I could visit often to help him get settled. There were many opportunities for him to work and he even started talking about enrolling at the community college. As the time drew nearer, his enthusiasm increased and I started thinking that maybe, just maybe, this was the time when he would finally be able to wipe away the destructive behavior of those early years and move forward with a new confidence and purpose. Other young people had survived turbulent, drug-laced years, and gone on to live full, productive and happy lives.

Cautiously, I allowed myself to get involved with his future plans.

Jamie.

Chapter Five

Twice Colombia, 2011

During the next two years, my attempt to sell my house consumed and influenced nearly all my actions. My recent trip to Cali had only fueled the desire to return and my friends there encouraged me to come back as soon as I could. Still not thoroughly convinced that I wanted to make a permanent move, I had no doubt that I wanted to spend more time there. I was so sure it would happen in a timely manner that I started preparing for the day when I could pack up everything and return to Colombia. But before that happened, I needed to finish my book, *Twice Colombia*.

I finally put myself on a schedule, just as if I were going to work. My workday started no later than nine o'clock when I sat down at the computer and did my most creative work. By that time I had showered, had breakfast, dressed and put on a small amount of make-up. Hair was also done. I worked until lunch time and did some stretching exercises before sitting down again in the afternoon. Afternoons were devoted to editing and rewriting and usually by four o'clock I was done. Working at night was never productive so I concentrated on the daytime hours.

When I took breaks, I cleaned out closets and gathered items to donate to favorite charities. My legal pad was always close by as I thought of people and businesses I would need to contact before I left. When clubs or organizations I belonged to called and asked for long term commitments, I declined.

The manuscript was taking shape and the original plan was to write about my time in Bogotá only. Writing about Cali, where I adopted my son Jamie, was not something I felt I could do yet. Perhaps later, so I plugged away on Bogotá.

I read about an upcoming seminar sponsored by the local Literacy Council entitled "Writing Memoirs" and signed up for it immediately. The person conducting the class, Dr. Susan Schmidt, was a published author and editor looking for work. After attending the one-day event, I felt that she might be someone with whom I could work. We met in May, 2010, for the first time to discuss my plans and her editing fees and after that, the book was off and running.

During the next six months I wrote and rewrote, and wrote some more. When Susan made suggestions, I usually always agreed but occasionally I bristled. I sat at my dining room table, bleary-eyed and bent over, and typed away. My body rebelled so I increased my Yoga workouts. Walking became my salvation when I needed to clear my head. My neighborhood of Trent Woods was a peaceful and lovely place to walk in the fall and winter of 2010 when I needed a change of scenery. With each step through the still somewhat remote area, I thought about what it would mean to me to give up this personal space. When my house sold, I knew I would experience a few withdrawal pains.

A former colleague, Richard McLawhorn, gave me the name of a publisher he had used for two of his self-published books and I started doing research on them and other publishers. Making the decision to self-publish freed me to concentrate on the writing. Had I been much younger, hoping to make a living at writing, I would have approached the publication differently. I finally decided on the one he recommended, Trafford Publishing, and prepared for the purchase of one of their packages. By Christmas, I was ready to make a commitment and finally bought a year-end, half-price, special deal. With money paid, there was no backing out now.

Susan had recommended that I add to the story by writing about my eighteen months in Cali.

"Susan, I don't think that's possible. How can I ever write about Jamie? That ended in such a painful manner and I'm not even sure I can remember enough to write about that experience," I said.

"Well, you can focus on Cali, instead of Jamie, and maybe something will develop," she countered. "What you have here isn't enough for a book." *If you hadn't cut so much from the original manuscript, it might be, I seethed, knowing she was right.*

And that's exactly how it started. I just jumped in and wrote a little about what happened in my life after I left Bogotá. Soon, I knew I had a wealth of information about the Cali friends I had met through the Friendship Force and that the story about them was worth telling. Jamie's memory was so intertwined in my relationship with the Platas and Francos and Colegio Bolívar, that within a few months, the Cali part was finished.

Publication

On December 31st, 2010, I submitted the manuscript to the publisher and felt that I was about to give birth. The real work with the book was still to come as the representatives of Trafford and I discussed the layout, the cover, the front and back write-ups and the information to give to Amazon for the digital edition. The proof rounds were endless and the more I looked at my sentences, the less I saw. My brain knew what was supposed to be there, but that didn't always translate into well-structured, error-free sentences. I also discovered that color is hard to discuss through e-mails. But all of this is the nature of self-publishing, and I knew that, for better or worse, there would soon be a book.

About six weeks later, the sample copy arrived and I held it as I would a fragile and delicate gift. The cover was lovely and I held my breath while opening the book and beginning to read. I was expecting typos, but nothing like the number I saw. I was horrified. As Richard McLawhorn had told me, "They'll print whatever you give them," and spellings that I, and my editor, had overlooked after countless readings, were there, just as they had been submitted. Words were omitted, apostrophes misplaced and at a certain point, I stopped reading. At other times, I picked it up, read chapters, and no errors jumped out.

During this time, a childhood friend, Willie Marlowe, who now lives in Albany, New York, had been supportive and encouraging. An accomplished and well-known artist, Willie always had the right words when I needed reassurance. As soon as the book was published and became available on Amazon, she was the first person to order a copy. Her review of the book sustained me for a long time.

Just as I was deciding how many books to order, or even if I wanted to order copies of this flawed book, a dear friend from high school, Linda Hufham, came for a visit. Linda lived in

Atlanta, Georgia, and we had stayed in touch through the years. She was a Spanish teacher and we had traveled together several times. When she and her husband, Toby, spent several summers in San Miguel de Allende, in Mexico, they never failed to invite me for a visit. Linda was always in my corner. She helped me find typos that I had overlooked and I started planning the second, improved edition.

Friends who stood by me during this time and understood my anxiety were my bedrock. Most of these friends were neither people I saw on a daily basis, nor ones I had worked with in New Bern. They were friends from an earlier time who had remained in touch, sometimes through Christmas cards or sometimes sympathy cards; they were always there when there was good news to share and didn't hesitate to offer congratulations when accomplishments were achieved. I felt blessed to have so many people supporting this effort, and at the same time, tried to understand that some people would never have an interest in the subject matter and would never say anything encouraging about the project. One person I had considered a friend even said "Who cares?" Another colleague told me one day that a friend of hers read the book, failing to mention whether or not she had read it herself. She never commented beyond that. I had no idea what point she was trying to make. I also prepared myself for the inevitable critics and tried to steel myself for their hurtful words. A former writing teacher told our class that after he published his first book, the critics were so vicious that he nearly put down his pen forever. Thankfully, he didn't do that and I kept that thought in mind as time went on. I also came across a quote from Jean Sibelius that said, "Pay no attention to what critics say; no statue has ever been put up to a critic." A sense of humor proved to be very therapeutic.

I ordered the books and started making plans to publicize it on my own. There were many local outlets and I took advantage of all the opportunities. I hand delivered complimentary copies to libraries, book stores, and places of business that might have an interest in a book about a young woman from the South who finds herself living on a plateau high in the Andes Mountains. New Bern was very supportive of local artists, of all genres, but the most popular books by area authors were those that had a local flavor. Mine didn't fall in that category, but I didn't let that hold me back. I signed up for several Saturdays at the local Farmers Market where writers, artists and others who had a "home grown" product could display their wares.

During the year that followed, calls and requests came in for speaking engagements and I prepared diligently for each presentation. I spoke to book clubs, civic organizations, gave readings, presented a travel program about Colombia, and was recognized by the New Bern and Havelock chapters of the American Association of University Women as one of ten local authors for the year. The Columbus County Arts Council hosted a reading and book signing in Whiteville, where I grew up, which was especially meaningful. Many friends of my parents still lived there and when I saw them I could easily imagine my mother and dad sitting among them in the audience listening to my story. A few high school friends showed up too, and I was thrilled. A book club presentation in Lake Waccamaw was attended mainly by women who knew and worked with my mother years ago. Nothing like Mom being there in spirit to offer support!

With each speech, I gradually got over my nearly paralyzing fear of public speaking. Speaking in front of a group of peers was a whole different ballgame than speaking in front of a class of teenagers. I realized that the key to it was thorough and precise preparation, along with practice – especially for me since I never considered myself to be a good extemporaneous speaker. That was one of the great personal benefits to come out of the entire publishing experience and I can comfortably give speeches now to anybody, anywhere, on nearly anything.

Another reward involved hearing from people I hadn't heard from or seen since high school or college days. I loved making contact with these people and was sorry it had taken so long to get together again. We had a lot to laugh and talk about and even managed to get together at the beach and other places for good visits.

The biggest surprise came from people who were total strangers who had found my book on the Internet when they were googling "Colombia," "teaching overseas," "international adoption," even "South America travel." Several of them wrote me directly and they always had positive things to say. They thanked me for sharing my story, wanted to know more about specific schools in Colombia and how to apply for jobs there. One middle-aged woman actually applied for a job that year and soon was accepted for a position in a small town outside Bogotá. Another woman and her husband had adopted a child from Russia and they were now waiting to adopt another child, this time from Colombia. Coincidentally, her husband was from Pamlico County which borders Craven County where New Bern is and where I live now. I heard from several people who had been in the Peace Corps who just wanted to make contact because they had shared similar experiences.

I often met people at the Farmers Market who had some connection to Colombia: a friend who had traveled there, a relative who lived there, or knew someone who married a Colombian. One sweet, elderly lady, accompanied by her younger neighbor, stopped by my table one day and told me she had been born in Colombia. She had married an Italian man and they settled in New Bern many years ago. She had no family here now and said she didn't have an e-mail address. She gave me her phone number and we made plans to have coffee one day. People who had lived overseas were the ones who really seemed to understand the pull of the expat's life and were the ones most eager to stay around for chats. I loved every minute of these engagements. If I happened to sell a few books, that was a bonus.

The most frequent and heartfelt comments, however, concerned my son Jamie. After expressing sympathy for my loss, they wanted to know more about him and hoped I would write his story someday. I gradually started thinking about that.

I can't say that all of this activity translated into big sales, but the book was moving. People requested copies from me directly and I mailed them out as soon as I could. A few copies went to my former schools in Colombia and also to my friends in Cali. Quarterly royalty checks came in, but my cut of any profit was minuscule and even though the eBooks were popular, I received even less for that format. I realized that without the support of a big publishing company I would not get rich and that was okay. At this time, I really had no interest in submitting manuscripts to publishers and was happy I wasn't trying to support a family with the profits. The reward couldn't be measured in dollar signs; it was measured in the heartfelt responses from friends and strangers alike.

Selling copies of *Twice Colombia* at the
Farmers Market in New Bern, 2011.

Listing House and Hurricane Irene

As soon as the initial activity with the publication of the book settled down, I moved forward with putting the house on the market. The timing couldn't have been worse. The real estate market was at an all-time low, but occasionally houses were selling and I was confident that soon mine would sell and I'd be able to move forward with my dream of returning to Colombia on a permanent basis.

With the help of a skilled and likable handyman, Larry Stauter, who took great pride in his work and who was really as much an artist as a handyman, the house was prepped and painted and renovated again. Larry was trustworthy and honest, and without his help, I could never have been ready to list the house so quickly. Clutter soon disappeared and fresh flowers appeared. It was a busy time and I was enjoying the activity. There were many showings, lots of good feedback, but the right buyer didn't come along.

And then, on the evening of Aug 26, 2011, I went to bed thinking that Hurricane Irene, which had been tracked for several days by meteorologists, was passing us by. I had experienced hurricanes many times in the past and felt that this one was gratefully going to spare us. Early on the morning of the 27th, however, I was awakened by the sound of the wind as it enveloped the pines and oaks in my yard. It was slow and steady and growing stronger in the early morning darkness. I had a sense of gusts of wind turning into swells of water at the beach. The rain started gently, but soon turned vicious as torrential amounts assaulted the house. I jumped out of bed and checked the power, which I still had, and ran to the kitchen to make coffee.

Losing power where I lived happened frequently during storms because of the vulnerability of the trees and above-ground power lines. They were easy targets for assaults by

Mother Nature and I knew firsthand what it was like to be without electricity. Fortunately, I had a gas stove and gas hot water heater, but the air conditioner and refrigerator were all electric. I was prepared for everything but didn't have a generator.

I heard the first transformer pop about an hour after I got up and everything went still and quiet inside. No a/c humming in the August heat, no TV reports from our local weatherman Skip about the hurricane and no lights to brighten the gray interior. Just the sound of Hurricane Irene. I heard lightning strike an old oak tree in my front yard and watched it split and fall into the overhead lines.

Candles were ready, food was available, and batteries were new. My cell phone was working and my sister Rachel, who also lives in New Bern, and I made contact. So now, I waited. The hurricane roared through the area during the day and by nightfall the skies had started to clear and the winds were calming. When I finally slept, I dreamed about earthquakes in Colombia.

As usual after a hurricane, the next day brought a pristine morning. I quickly went outside to assess the damage and was relieved that no major harm was done to my house. From the many trees in the yard, there were branches down and yard debris, the big oak was lying in the front yard, and the old telephone wires were ripped from the side of the house. I gingerly stepped around my property, being ever alert for critters that usually showed up when the wind and rain caused the water level in the river to rise. If snakes and turtles were seeking refuge here, I didn't see them then.

Clean up efforts were massive and ongoing in the affected counties for a long time and there was no electricity on my block for five days. I finally threw out frozen foods and took the opportunity to clean out my refrigerator thoroughly. The real estate market tanked. My realtor suggested that I take my house off the market and I complied immediately and set about doing what I could to make my property presentable again. I also reexamined my plans to move to Colombia and realized that, if I still wanted to do that, I was in for the long haul. There was no pressure from anywhere to make a decision, so I continued to make my plans carefully for the move.

Ximena's Heart Attack and Relisting the House

In early September, 2011, I received a message from Margarita, Ximena and Rafael's younger daughter, that Ximena had suffered a heart attack. She had just undergone open heart surgery. The surgery was successful and she was resting comfortably in Intensive Care. The news was shocking and I regretted very much that I was not closer so I could help her family. She was like a sister to me and I was very concerned about her well-being. Her family stayed in touch during the entire ordeal, and I was relieved in October to receive an email from Ximena herself indicating that she was improving daily. Her days were filled with doctor appointments, physical therapy, and resting at home. She expressed much gratitude for being alive and was extremely appreciative for all the prayers sent to her via Rafael, María Isabel and Margarita. When she started asking about my plans to return to Colombia and then later saying she was looking for a new car, I was confident she was on the road to recovery.

With the help of Larry, my faithful handyman, I moved forward with plans to renovate and improve my house. I continued with my activities related to the book and looked forward to the time when I could list my house again. I became involved with St. Cyprian's Episcopal Church at a time when they needed some help and I volunteered a lot of time to that effort. It kept me occupied. I didn't know I was forming special friendships and bonds when I first showed up there, but their presence in my life became a precious and cherished consequence of my staying in New Bern while waiting for my house to sell. I valued their gift of friendship and respected their unique history in New Bern and Craven County.

In November, I received an email from Isa, Esteban and Marta's daughter, that she and Pablo were getting married in June. She said she would send more information soon. Happy for them, I started looking forward to the wedding and hoped I'd be able to go.

Meanwhile, my activities with the book continued, which included another presentation to a book club in New Bern. I had been asked to discuss my inspiration for writing the book and was always thrilled to discuss anything related to the book's development. Of the ten people present, I knew two of them: Dr. Murdina MacDonald, a friend and former Spanish professor, and another woman who was also a member of a club to which I belonged. The others were from many places around the United States. Most were retired, had traveled extensively, and had chosen New Bern as their retirement home. They were actively involved in community affairs and supported local arts and artists. After my presentation, they asked thoughtful questions and related some of their own experiences with travel in South America and international adoptions. And, then, in what was probably meant to be a very kind remark, one of them said, "Whoever would have thought that a little country girl like you would go off and do something like this?" I was momentarily stunned.

That kind of attitude was something I ran into in Bogotá from North Americans and it always made me bristle. My thought was, "What does she mean by "a little country girl?" and why does she think I'm a little country girl? There was nothing in the book to indicate that I was a "country girl" in a sense that I understood, and so, all I could surmise was that she thought all Southerners were "country people." I never took that kind of comment as a compliment because I didn't think they had a clue what a "country person" was. Country people are deserving of the greatest respect, but she obviously had a misconception about people from the South and I couldn't help feeling defensive. It was as if she were implying that Southerners don't travel and are not educated. Yak, yak, yak. I had addressed that in the book and tried to ignore her comment. The person leading the discussion moved on and nothing else was said about "country girls." Do you think I was a little sensitive? She could have retired up North, you know? I think I was just needing to blow off some steam.

By March of 2012, I was ready to put my house back on the market. Indicators were that sales were picking up, if ever so slightly, and with spring coming, I thought it would be the right time to try again. I had done all I could do to prepare for the move to Colombia and would now have to wait for the actual sale before checking anything else off my list. I hired a new agent, Kelly Latimer, of Trent Woods Realty, and prepared for showings. She was attentive and professional, and always well prepared.

Around this time, I received the official wedding invitation from Isa. She and Pablo were finally getting married on June 2, 2012, and she hoped I could come. There was no question about my attending, but I had really hoped I would be living in Cali by that time and not just visiting. There was still time, I told myself, for the house to sell so I could make the move, but that didn't happen. There were encouraging showings but the right buyer still didn't come along.

Ximena and I continued to correspond, and in one e-mail she told me she wanted to translate *Twice Colombia* into Spanish. She was excited about the prospect and felt that the book would be popular in Colombia. The more I thought about it, the more I agreed. After all, this was a book that was complimentary to the Colombian people and their culture. I had deliberately stayed away from politics and tried to focus on the people who were living in a society that didn't often read positive things about their lives – especially written by North Americans. So we agreed on a price for the translation and Ximena hoped to have it finished by the time I arrived for Isa's wedding. Apparently, this was something she could do while still recovering from her heart attack.

As I continued my patient waiting, I found plenty to keep me busy. I continued with my work at St. Cyprian's and with book-related activities. When concerts featuring favorite performers such as Diana Krall at DPAC in Durham were scheduled, I took full advantage of them. When my great-niece Caitlin Little was performing in a college play in Chicago, I found a reasonably-priced deal online and went to see her. Reconnecting with old friends became an activity I joyfully embraced, but Cali was always on the back burner. There were times when I was beginning to question my decision to move, but I never questioned my decision to sell my house. It was time to down-size whether I stayed in New Bern or moved to Colombia and I was committed to doing just that.

A lovely spring arrived early in eastern North Carolina and on May 29, 2012, I once again departed for Cali. I packed special clothes to wear to Isa's wedding and hoped they would be appropriate for the outdoor event at Lake Calima. My thoughts about moving were changing, but with my house still on the market, I didn't have to make a definite decision. I looked forward to visiting with friends in Colombia again. I wanted to concentrate on enjoying the trip and take time to think about my relationship with Colombia.

Jamie – New Start

In the weeks before Jamie's release, I bought him a few new clothes, gathered information about Cape Fear Community College in Wilmington, looked in the want ads for possible jobs and found information about the homeless shelter. Jamie understood that I could not provide an apartment for him and we agreed that staying at the shelter while he got settled would be his only option for housing.

Early in the morning on May 29, 2000, I packed a few of his things in the car and drove to Maury where I was told to pick him up after 10:00 a.m. It was a somber and reflective drive, but the time passed quickly and the knot in my stomach slowly subsided. The weather was beautiful and still cool with the early morning brightness and clarity of a sun-kissed day. I knew the scenery on our drive to Wilmington would be a welcome respite from the walls of the prison after more than two years and I anticipated that he would be a reserved, but cooperative passenger on this trip.

There was little fanfare as I announced myself at the gate and then walked into a waiting room to sit while he was prepared for dismissal. When he finally came in the small room, we smiled at each other and I stood up to quietly hug him. Papers were signed, he was given a small bag of personal belongings and a few comments were exchanged.

As we walked, side by side, to the car, I barely recognized him. He had changed and he didn't seem like the boy I once knew. I thought of all the times we had walked together in Cali, from the apartment to Cosmo Centro, from the school bus up the stairs to the apartment, from the movie theater to a taxi, always with him walking a little behind me. People said he did that so he could see me and keep up with me better. Today, he was still walking a little behind me.

On the way to Wilmington, we stopped for lunch at a barbeque restaurant and he filled up. There wasn't much conversation, but there was no hostility and the mood was pleasant. I think neither one of us knew what to expect, but we moved through the day with open minds.

The first thing we did when we arrived in Wilmington was stop by the mall where I bought him shoes. The ones he was wearing were heavy, state-issued brogans and they looked like prison shoes. After another quick stop at a grocery store where we bought fruit and crackers, we went to the shelter. I had been in touch with the director there and knew that he would have a bed and meals. A thrift shop was on the premise and we picked up a few items of clothing. During the day, he could pursue jobs close by, and hopefully, be hired soon. The employees at the shelter were kind and supportive, and I think he felt comfortable. He knew he could call me collect if he needed to and when I left, he was preparing to go to the Pizza Hut to fill out an application.

Fortunately, he was hired soon and by all accounts, was a responsible and hard worker. He showed up on time and soon was given a raise. He became friends with some of the other young people who worked there, most of them college students, and made plans to move into an apartment with two of them. One of his first purchases was a bicycle which allowed him to move around the city and soon he had a girlfriend. I visited him about once a week, and after he moved out of the shelter, helped him with groceries and household items for a while.

He called one day and said he wanted me to meet the girlfriend on my next trip and said we could go to her house for lunch. She lived in a trailer, was a single parent, had one child and worked in a gift shop in the mall. I was not surprised he had found someone so quickly and just hoped she would be supportive and a good influence on him. He seemed content.

I picked him up at his apartment and we drove to the trailer park. As trailer parks go, it was not too shoddy. When we walked in, I was surprised to meet a woman at least ten years older than he – he was twenty-three now - and her son was about twelve. She was pleasant enough and we had a nice, if somewhat awkward, lunch of ham and cheese sandwiches with lettuce and tomato, chips and iced tea. For dessert, she had baked cookies. We didn't stay long because Jamie had to get to work and as we were driving back to his apartment, he told me that they had been dating a while and she had recently had an abortion. She'd had a tubal ligation which apparently was not successful so the pregnancy was a surprise to both of them. I never knew what to say to Jamie when he told me these intimate details, and he had always done that. So, today I just listened and commented very little, saying only that, yes, that surgery was not always one hundred percent effective. The relationship lasted a few more months and I never heard anything else about her.

We continued to visit through the following months, sometimes with Mother going along, and on Christmas Day I went to his new apartment in Wilmington. He had found a small efficiency in one of the old, historic homes in the downtown area and received a reduction in rent by helping the owner of the house with minor repairs and lifting and carrying large objects. He had found a small Christmas tree and decorated it with items he found in a thrift shop. He had always enjoyed cooking and that day he prepared a lunch of boxed pasta and sauce, instant rice and canned string beans. The pasta was placed on top of the rice which was a combination probably deeply embedded in his memory from his days in Colombia. He set the small table correctly and artistically, and was very proud of being able to cook for me. I enjoyed the attention and let him know how much I appreciated his efforts. We exchanged presents after lunch and spent a relaxing afternoon together talking about many things. We talked about his job, his plans to apply for admission to Cape Fear Tech after the holidays, and we also talked about Colombia. He always liked for me to tell him stories about some of the funny things he did when we lived there and it was very poignant for both of us. I treasured these times because I felt it was important for him to maintain his cultural identity and what better way to do that than recalling events we had shared there. Also, the memories of those good times, for me, were therapeutic and tender. I still loved him very much and I think he felt the same about me. He didn't remember any Spanish, but was beginning to express an interest in the language. I also wanted to make sure that he didn't forget the struggle we went through to get him to the States. We called it "our lesson in love and perseverance." He told me about a new girlfriend who was closer to his age than the previous one. The new one also had a child. When I left around 4 p.m. to return to New Bern, I felt encouraged by his behavior and demeanor. A heavy weight seemed to have lifted from his shoulders, as well as mine, and I felt a catch in my throat a few times on the way home as I remembered our journey together.

During the following winter months, the girlfriend and the baby moved in with Jamie, and I knew he was having financial problems. Whenever I visited, the first thing we did was go to the grocery store and buy staples which they all needed. Jamie was generous and wanted to provide for the girl and her child, but had not learned about budgeting or the financial responsibilities of being an adult. I think she had a part-time job which helped pay for a few items, but it didn't begin to cover her fair share. We talked about setting up a budget to help him and he sounded interested, but we never got around to it. I lent him a small amount of money, but it wasn't enough to keep up with his expenses, and even though he made partial payments to me, he never seemed to get ahead. My big concern at that time was that she would get pregnant and then we'd have a whole new set of problems to deal with. He assured me they were taking precautions, but I never stopped worrying about that.

I was not surprised when he called one Wednesday night and said that she had moved out. He sounded genuinely upset and I did what I could to offer him comfort. We talked for a long time and made plans to get together a week from Saturday when I would go to the apartment and pick him up and we'd go out to eat. The coming weekend I would be taking part in a program in New Bern on Saturday and wouldn't be able to go to Wilmington. It was then that he told me he had given up the apartment and had moved in with three guys he had met. They were sharing a large apartment in another house in the downtown area. There was something about the whole arrangement that sounded suspicious. Maybe it was because he couldn't tell me much about his roommates or didn't say how long he had known them. Maybe it was his tone of voice which seemed to have lost some of the confidence and maturity I thought he had recently shown. Whatever it was, it set off alarms. When he said "I'll be able to pay you back your money this weekend," I knew something was wrong. For him to have extra money after what he had been dealing with - the girlfriend and child, and the expenses in the apartment - just didn't make sense. Before hanging up, I mentioned something about being careful in choosing who he was hanging out with, and to take good care of himself. I told him I loved him, he told me the same thing and I said, "I'll see you in a week. Bye, sweetie."

"Bye, Mom."

Chapter Six

Cali, Summer 2012

Wedding Preparations

Manicure, pedicure, hair, makeup, and false eyelashes! All for approximately $40 US. At a time when a basic manicure and pedicure, even in a small Southern town in the States, could run more than $50, the notion of indulging in those luxuries on the day of Isa's wedding at Lake Calima was irresistible. Ximena had written me before the trip to say that we could do it all on the day of the ceremony and that a woman would come to her apartment to get us ready. "Yes," I responded, "let's do it!"

However, by the time we arrived in Lake Calima for the wedding, around noon and two hours from Cali, the manis and pedis were a day old, hair and makeup, for me, were a disaster, and there were no new eyelashes for anybody.

When Ximena made our original appointments with the beautician, she anticipated there would be just the two of us receiving the services. But a few days before the wedding, Ximena found out that her daughter, Margarita, and Margarita's daughter, Salomé, would spend the night before the wedding in the apartment with us and they would also need hair and makeup done. With not enough time for just one person to take care of all of us in the morning, we had manicures and pedicures done the day before and washed our own hair on the day of the wedding. That would leave hair styling and makeup for the hired stylist, Ramona. We'd have to forego the eyelashes.

I knew there would be problems when we all gathered in the living room and Ximena requested a classic updo and Ramona said she preferred doing a different style. Ximena acquiesced and it looked fine, but I could tell she wasn't happy. Ramona worked on Margarita and Salomé, with satisfactory results and then it was my turn. My hair is different from the thick, black (or silver), straight, glossy hair of my Colombian friends, but I had had good results previously getting a wash and blow dry in different beauty parlors in Colombia. The beauticians had been up to date on the latest styles and they knew how to handle my thin, silver/blond, slightly wavy tresses and I was looking forward to similar results on this day. I certainly wasn't expecting a big swoop in front, reminiscent of days gone by, anchored down with a hefty dose of hair spray. My friends said it was glamorous. They were being nice and I was horrified.

Next came the makeup which, for me, was even more inappropriate. Ramona knew how to apply makeup to the Colombian women with their beautiful, café au lait skin and black eyebrows and eyelashes. She used her makeup kit expertly and deftly to create an alluring and sophisticated look, even for six-year-old Salomé, who was one of the flower girls in the wedding. By the time she had finished with them and it was my turn, I had decided I would do my own makeup.

"Ramona, I have makeup and I don't mind applying it myself. I really don't use very much and I think the colors I have might be better."

"Oh, Patricia, I think you just want a more natural look, right?"

I nodded and mumbled "Yes."

"I can do that," she insisted and before I could come up with another excuse, I was in her chair and she was experimenting with colors. After seeing the new lilac-colored pashmina shawl I would be wearing to the wedding she went to work. I couldn't see what she was doing, but I could feel the foundation, powder, blush, eye shadow, liquid eyeliner and, most frightening of all, a brush on my eyebrows. Makeup is nothing new to me and I love to try new looks, but one thing that has stayed the same over the years has been my pale eyebrows. A little shaping and a little color and I'm done. But never a thick, dark, brow brushed in. It's just not becoming on me. When I saw the finished project I was speechless and near tears. All I could do was stare and wonder how I could go to this special wedding looking like a clown. Ramona, however, either was thrilled with her work or covering up the disaster with sighs of approval. All I could do was pay her, excuse myself as quickly as possible, and get out of that room.

There wasn't time to repair the hair, but I did manage to soften the eyebrows a bit. I decided at that moment that I would do everything I could to avoid photographers and hoped that nobody snapped any pictures of me that would end up on Facebook. I also reminded myself that the wedding was not about me.

The five of us packed up the new Renault with our party clothes and overnight bags and started out on the two hour trip to Lake Calima. We made a quick stop at Esteban and Marta's house on the lake, where the wedding would be, to let them know we had arrived with the flower girl. There were many people, mostly family, milling about and enjoying their lunch and the festive occasion. Several women, some who looked just like Marta, were putting the finishing touches on the outdoor site where the ceremony would take place and a few men were setting up the sound equipment on a small stage. Everybody was focused on the wedding.

Marta and Esteban's restaurant, *Meson Ilama*, was next door to the house and preparations were well under way for the reception to come later. Family members and out-of-town guests were settling into the cozy cabanas or rooms which were a part of the restaurant complex and children had already made their way to the swimming pool. A few dogs were happily scampering about, taking part in all the activities. From the lake front, one could clearly see the wind surfers against the backdrop of the mountains and I mentally calculated that the clouds and wind would arrive in a few hours, just in time for the wedding.

We soon left the Plata's house and made the short drive to *La Casa Azul,* the blue house, where Maria Isabel and her family were waiting for us. Maria Isabel, Ximena and Rafael's older daughter, and her family - her husband, Dr. Hernan Muñoz (Mellizo), their two sons, Juan Miguel age fifteen and José Tomás age eight - were there to welcome us. The same maid I had met previously, Esmeralda, was busy in the kitchen and two new Labrador Retriever puppies, Bruno and Tina, had joined the household. Rolfo, their older lab, was still walking around with a huge banana leaf in his mouth.

In the two years since I had visited Lake Calima, the Muñoz family had built a guest house on their property which included one bedroom and bath and a large covered patio area complete with pool table, sofas and chairs, and kitchen equipment. Orange and mango trees, impatiens, vinca, hydrangea and many other lush plants had been carefully landscaped and were cared for by a gardener. Esmeralda helped in the yard when needed. The smooth, round stones that we paid so much for in eastern North Carolina, outlined pathways and flower beds and came from the rivers. Close by was a full outdoor kitchen where Rafael soon started preparing the classic Colombian soup, *Sancocho,* with fish – bass - instead of chicken. We settled into our spaces in the house while he was cooking and soon ate a filling and satisfying lunch. We knew the wedding celebration could go on for a long time that evening so everybody took a short siesta before starting the final preparations for the ceremony.

The Ceremony

Promptly at 4 o'clock, Ximena, Rafael and I turned off the tree-lined, two-lane, country road to the Plata's house, passed through the manned gate, and followed the hand painted signs to the wedding site. Down the curving, dirt and gravel driveway to the parking area - and spectacular view of the lake – Rafael skillfully avoided the potholes and slowly pulled the car onto a grassy knoll. The winds and clouds would come soon, but at that moment, the panorama was a precious glimpse of serene, heavenly perfection.

Uniformed guards with automatic firearms, inside and outside the gate, seemed to crackle with intensity like exploding fireworks. It was a sobering reminder that even though security issues in Colombia had improved in recent years, there was still a need to provide protection at events like this, when well-to-do families gathered in celebration. My mind was firing missives, saying, "Don't forget, don't let your guard down, check over your shoulder, remember the red *ruana* incident in Bogotá" and then, "Enjoy the party."

A sea of black and white, with vivid splashes of color, provided a stunning backdrop as we approached the wedding party. From the emerald green of the grassy hill leading to the covered cabana by the lake where the bridal couple would take their vows, framed by pale, Carolina blue skies, to the black and silver gleaming hair of the guests already milling about, to the splendid white of the traditional *guayabera* shirts and pants the men were wearing, to the women's designer dresses in silks and satins in black and white or shimmering colors, it was visual stimulation and entertainment. I could easily identify the paternal side of the bride's family – some of whom I had never met - by their tall, aristocratic good looks passed down through generations from their Spanish ancestors. The maternal side was easy to spot, too, and they all resembled Marta, the mother of the bride. While I had met the groom-to-be two years earlier, I had never met his family, but they, too, had their distinct look. Of varying heights, their coloring was lighter and bespoke their Scandinavian roots.

Ximena explained that there were basically five groups of people at the wedding: the maternal and paternal lines from the bride and groom and then, friends not related. Clearly, I fell into the last group. When we were told it was time to gather for the ceremony I was surprised and honored to be ushered to the seats reserved for close family. There were gleaming, wooden benches in front of the cabana for about eighty people and that was where I sat. The rest of the guests stood behind the benches and higher up the incline.

By this time, almost 4:30 p.m., the clouds had begun to quickly roll in: at first, small, white and puffy. The wind picked up, and within minutes, the view of the mountains and much of the lake was obscured. I wondered why the couple had chosen to have the ceremony at this particular time, knowing what the weather would be like, but I realized later that probably no place on earth at 4:30 p.m. was more symbolic and special to them. During their eight-year courtship, Isa and Pablo had spent many hours on the lake, and this weather phenomenon that happened each day was as much a part of their lives here as the predictable love and support of their families. The lake, the clouds, the wind, were all part of a time capsule for them and would forever define this moment. Also, Isa had said they wanted a typical, Colombian, country wedding. So maybe this was a part of that.

At the end of each bench, on the center aisle, were decorations of three glass bottles, full of different colored shasta daisies. Tied with colorful ribbons, they cascaded down the side of the benches and were fresh and bright. The wooden canopy, where the couple would take their vows, was adorned with more flowers and was gracefully draped in a muslin fabric. As the wind increased, the artistic display became an evolving visual spectacle. Two ornate, wooden chairs, passed down through generations in the bride's family, were placed in front of the altar for the bride and groom to use during the ceremony. They were gleaming and appeared to be mahogany.

"These are from my mother's family," Ximena whispered to me as we waited for the ceremony to begin. I remembered her mother, Nora, well, and knew she would be proud and happy on this special day.

Soon, the priest, smiling jovially, and the groom, Pablo, looking anxious, appeared and the musicians took their places. With the wind now whipping and hair flying, the guests braced themselves and stood when the music started, and the procession began. First, Pablo's parents stepped carefully from the top of the hill down the stone steps beside the benches, followed by Marta, the mother of the bride, escorted by a family member. Close behind were Sofía, Isa's younger sister and maid of honor, and then the two flower girls and ring bearer. Sofía must have grown six inches since I saw her two years earlier and I barely recognized her in her sophisticated, sexy gown with a deep split up the side. Then came the bride, Isa, and her father, my dear friend, Esteban. Isa was elegant and serene in a simple classic gown and Esteban was justly proud. I remembered a trip to this very same spot many years ago when Isa was an infant and Esteban and Marta had not yet built their house here. I had not adopted my son, Jamie, yet but that event was on the horizon and Esteban and Marta were a huge part of that experience. Never did I imagine at that time that nearly thirty years later, our lives would be so intertwined. I momentarily visualized what my son, Jamie, would look like now and knew that he would be indistinguishable from the other Colombians here. He would also be considered a member of this family, and tall and handsome, with thick dark hair, I knew he'd be garnering his own attention.

The stone walkway curved around behind the benches and then unfolded down the center aisle. Once the wedding party was in place, we were all instructed to take our seats. As we settled in, the fierce wind continued and I pulled out my new, lilac, pashmina shawl. I was actually enjoying the wind because, even though I knew my hair was standing straight out and up, I felt that it had to be an improvement over the disastrous hairdo I'd been given earlier that morning.

I've been to a few Catholic weddings in the States and this wedding appeared to be a typical, Catholic wedding. The ceremony was informal and convivial with much conversing among the bridal couple, their families and the priest. Not able to follow the entire service in Spanish, my mind wandered to my first trip to Lake Calima in 1982 and the discovery of this very special place. Created in the 1940s as part of a hydroelectric project to generate power for the Cauca Valley, it is a favorite weekend get-away for people in neighboring towns. Surrounded by mountains at nearly 5,000 feet, it is a cool and refreshing retreat and has become a popular tourist destination. Windsurfing and water skiing are important sports here, and I remembered water skiing in this same lake many years ago with some of the same family members I was with today – and before Isa, the bride, was born.

From where I was sitting at the wedding, I could see a lone windsurfer on the edge of the water. Perhaps unaware that a wedding was taking place, he performed his graceful ballet of turns and dives as the wind propelled him along. About halfway through the ceremony, a mixed-breed stray dog walked down the aisle, looked around and sat down in front of the priest, who made a comment which I didn't understand, but which was apparently appreciated, since the entire congregation laughed. The dog remained there until the ceremony was over and was very well-behaved. Later, I found out that no one knew who he belonged to, but somehow, he had found his way to the wedding.

Clouds enveloped Isa and Pablo, almost on cue, as they kissed, and promised everlasting love. The wedding ended with much cheering and hand-clapping. When firecrackers went off after the last blessing, however, several of us momentarily turned with apprehension as we looked up the hill expecting to see uzi-toting guerillas storming the property. It was all a joke, we were told, and I held judgment on the humor of such a prank. I wasn't the only one who felt a little uneasy. For Isa and Pablo, however, it was their day, and the festivities were just beginning.

Isa and Pablo

The Reception

The bride and groom led the way up the hill from the banks of the river to tables set up on the lawn with refreshments. As soon as they started up the walkway, the musicians began playing happy, salsa music. Squealing with delight, the children scampered around the bridal couple and raced to the top. Guests chatted and laughed and everyone seemed caught up in the excitement and anticipation. A professional photographer moved among the crowd taking candid shots and many of us had our own cameras. The Colombians could have all been professional models; they were so striking looking.

The country theme continued with the choice of food for this part of the wedding. I had noticed over the years that many Colombians were becoming more health conscious and aware of the need to ease up on the heavy fried foods that were so typical of their culture – and so tasty! But for this part of the wedding, the traditional country foods took center stage, and I was determined to taste everything.

Xavier, one of Esteban's brothers and Isa's youngest uncle, was in charge of the food and had created a drink and four dishes typical of the Cauca Valley. The drink, *lulada*, was made from the juice of the *lulo* fruit, peeled, chopped finely but with chunky bits left, and mixed with a little sugar and water. It was served in glasses with spoons, was green, and tasted a lot better than it looked - refreshing and tart.

The first dish I tasted was *maranitas. Platano verdes,* green bananas, were mixed with corn meal and a small piece of fried pork and egg, shaped into rounds and then cooked outside in a vat of hot oil. Crispy and hot, they were placed on a paper napkin to drain and to be enjoyed immediately. They reminded me of hush puppies from the South.

The next dish was another banana-based treat, but this one called for the sweet, mature, banana – the ones which always appeared way past their expiration date to me, but were, in fact, sweet and very edible. *Aborrajados* were prepared using two slices of the banana. A piece of cheese is placed on top of one slice and the second piece of banana is placed on top of that. The edges are pinched together to seal and then they are dipped in eggs beaten with flour before being dropped in the hot oil just long enough to melt the cheese inside. Served fresh they are filling and delicious – fruit and cheese at their best.

Tostadas were next and were made from the green bananas again, sliced, fried and seasoned with a little salt. An *hogado* sauce, made with tomato, green onions, and a little paprika, was served with the crispy *tostadas*. These were similar to potato chips.

The final dish, one of my long time favorites and the one I was most familiar with were the *empanadas*, little fried cornmeal pies stuffed with a variety of fillings - cheese, pork or beef and served with a *chimichurri* sauce, made with cilantro, green onions, garlic, and a little vinegar and water. No one seemed to mind when the sauce ran down their arms.

After tasting all the dishes, I was sated and knew I'd had my share of cholesterol and fat for the year. It was still early, the wind had calmed down and the clouds were moving out. The cool air had appeared on the wings of the setting sun. It was the time of day at Lake Calima when silver rivulets adorned everything – the water, the mountains, and the houses along the river banks. My shawl felt warm, and as we moved up the hill to the restaurant next door, I couldn't imagine what else was in store. I knew the Colombians well enough to expect music and dancing eventually, but I was not expecting another round of food on a jaw-dropping scale.

I had eaten at Esteban's restaurant, *Meson Ilama*, several times and always looked forward to the rustic atmosphere and good food. I loved the casual ambience and the conversations that took place there, usually among people of all ages and all backgrounds. He and some of his brothers owned and managed the property, which included small rental cabins as well as the restaurant. They had invested a lot of time and personal sweat equity in the operation and décor. On the night of the wedding, the chalet-style building with open wooden beams was decorated colorfully, creatively and extensively. Multi-level stone floors were full of tables seating eight to twelve, covered with white tablecloths and avocado green runners. Hand printed place cards were at every seat, along with white cloth napkins, gleaming silverware, and wine, water, and champagne glasses. Each table was adorned with vases of flowers and candles, creating a romantic, elegant atmosphere. Tucked into nooks around the room and hanging from the beams were massive displays of more fresh flowers.

Around the perimeter of the restaurant were antiques, many of which had been restored by Javier. To the right as one entered the building was a table with an old-fashioned, manual typewriter. A note from Isa and Pablo asking guests to type a message for them was on the table and people were doing just that. Some of the younger people had, no doubt, never typed on a typewriter. There were old radios, a victrola, even an ancient-looking dentist's chair. Early television sets, record players for 45 rpm records, water filters, farm tools, and hand-made baskets were among the many artifacts. Everything was from the Cauca Valley and when the original owners of the items were known, their names were given in the description. Nestled among the museum-quality displays were small vases of flowers, or for the larger items, potted plants. Candles adorned the display areas and cast an almost eerie glow. Earthenware jars of varying heights and shapes were placed on steps leading to the different levels. One could easily spend an hour or two just looking at these artifacts which had been carefully gathered and arranged for this event. Most guests took at least one tour during the evening. What is it about the past that grabs our interest and makes us long for insight into a way of life in a different era? Even though I didn't have the same connection to these items that most people here had, there was no doubt that the North American versions had an important place in my own history.

Ximena, Rafael and I walked in together and were immediately escorted to our table where we each found our name cards. My seat was at one end of the table and provided a clear view of all the activity. Other family members were seated with us and at tables close by. Of the nine siblings in Esteban's family, eight were at the wedding with their spouses or companions. Many of Isa's cousins were there, but most of their generation were seated in a different area, closer to the dance floor.

Approximately an hour after arriving and finding our seats, waiters appeared with our choice of red or white wine. I don't know for sure and couldn't tactfully ask the waiters, but I'm pretty sure we were drinking malbecs and chardonnays from Argentina. Wine was as popular in Colombia as it was in the States, and from the Chilean wines in Bogotá many years ago to the high quality wines available today, I was looking forward to having such a wide variety available when I moved there. Unfortunately, the Colombian wines would probably never seriously compete with these because of the lack of a real change of seasons, which grapes need to produce fine wines.

The wine worked its magic and people began meandering around the room full of high spirits and good will. When Isa and Pablo appeared, following their photo session, the members of the wedding party were ready to celebrate. Champagne was brought around, and amid cheers and music, the bridal couple was toasted by family and friends. I could hear the speeches from the back of the room but couldn't understand. There was no denying, however, that jokes were made and people were ready to celebrate. Just like weddings back home. It was soon time for Isa and Pablo to start the dancing, which was slow and romantic in the beginning, and then Esteban, Marta, and the groom's family joined in. When the obligatory dances had taken place in the proper order, the music shifted gears and others joined in to the lively, fun, salsa sounds.

As I watched the guests, young and old, dance, it seemed to me that everybody was an expert dancer. Facial expressions changed and years seemed to fade away - from those old enough to have a few years to shed! I had always thought the salsa was very similar to the dance I grew up with, the shag, from the coastal areas of North and South Carolina. Similar in that, once learned, nobody ever forgot how to do it. Some of the guests were older than I and they were dancing like teenagers. Once learned, either salsa or shag, it was a part of you forever and that night, I wanted to shag and experience that exhilaration again. Flying around a dance hall doing the Polka, as my boyfriend and I did in Germany many years ago, flashed through my mind, too, and I suddenly missed that boyfriend. I watched the faces of those dancing and they were illuminated by pure joy. When Xavier asked me to dance, I was grateful. He's an expert dancer and had patiently guided me around the dance floor a long time ago when I was trying to find my salsa beat. I can't really say my salsa skills have improved as much as I'd like, but it was fun to dance and feel I could hold my own on the dance floor. I made a mental note to think about trying to find someone in Cali who knew how to shag.

At 9 p.m. waiters passed the word that dinner was being served, buffet style. It didn't seem possible that we could be hungry again, but after a few hours of dancing and a few glasses of wine, appetites were whetted. This time, there was nothing fried in sight. Waiters in long-sleeved white shirts and black ties were lined up behind a candle-lit, beautifully appointed table, preparing plates as guests passed through the line. The first dish was broiled chicken breasts with a lemon, curry sauce sprinkled with rosemary. A beef in mushroom sauce entree was next and I chose both the chicken and beef since I always liked to try the different dishes and I noticed that most people were doing the same. Farther down, another server artfully piped creamed potatoes through a pastry bag beside the two meats on my plate and the final dish was stir fried vegetables – squash, zucchini, carrots, onions - in a ginger Thai sauce. The vegetables were my favorite part of the menu, but all of the dishes had been skillfully prepared.

We took our time enjoying this delicious meal and waiters continued hovering close by with wine - or water, which many of us were drinking now. The musicians continued playing while we ate, and as people finished their meals and pushed their plates aside, waiters cleared the tables. Soon slices of the bride's cake were brought around. A light, luscious chocolate, it was more like a mousse and it was exquisite. For those who wanted coffee, waiters brought it and we capped off the meal perfectly.

People were soon stretching their legs by walking around the room, visiting other guests and looking at the antiques again. Some were already back on the dance floor while the music switched to a louder, pulsing beat and the night moved on. After the few children at the reception were rounded up and taken home, waiters appeared again, this time with *aguardiente,* the Colombian alcoholic drink distilled from the sugar cane. Strong and licorice-flavored and often served mixed with juice or cola, tonight it was just the bottles placed on the tables. I have no idea how they drank it because, at 10:30 p.m., I was on my way back to *la casa azul,* the blue house. As I left, I could see the bottles being opened at the tables.

Within an hour, Ximena and Rafael arrived back at the house and said that as soon as I left, the band started playing Rock and Roll music. I'm sorry I didn't get to hear it and watch the young people and the dances they were doing. We were soon all in bed and I, at least, was sound asleep almost before my head hit the pillow. I have no idea what time the others got in, but Esteban told us later that he closed and locked the restaurant at 3:30 a.m. So that was a typical Colombian wedding.

The Party Ends

Sunday began and ended as a day of rest. For breakfast, Esmeralda prepared *arepas* with eggs. She rolled and flattened the mass of corn meal and water to a certain thickness and then dropped them in a frying pan full of hot oil. When they started rising on top, she removed them quickly, opened them with a sharp knife, and dropped an egg inside with a little butter. She then closed the edges and returned the *arepas* to the frying pan for a few more minutes for the eggs to cook. We had papaya juice and coffee with the *arepas* as we relaxed around the dining room table.

As soon as we were able to move about, Ximena and I went for a walk in a dense, wooded, hilly area where hikers often trekked. To me, it appeared very jungle-like with the tall trees, heavy vegetation and only the occasional ray of sunshine piercing through the overhangs. A local dog, who belonged to one of the guards on the property, went with us and proved to be an able guide. When we veered too far in one direction and couldn't get through because of the undergrowth, he led us in another direction. There were fresh horse tracks and horse droppings all along the way, but we didn't see or hear anybody riding. Fallen trees provided easy access across creeks, and Ximena and I whooped and hollered as we tried to avoid sliding off the moss-covered limbs into the water. We laughed when she told me that Pablo Escobar and his cohorts used to ride their horses here back in the eighties. I imagine they found it to be fine sport.

After a couple of hours, we were ready to think about escaping the woods, and with the help of the dog, began our trek back to the house. We had to backtrack a few times, but finally came to a clearing. A nearly invisible barbed wire fence appeared just before we plowed right into it and eventually we had to crawl on our stomachs like snakes to get under it. A yellow fruit had fallen to the ground where we were slithering and when we finally stood up, we noticed that our clothes and shoes were covered in a yellow stain. A permanent souvenir, we surmised.

Back at the house, people were getting ready to go out for a late lunch. Ximena and I showered and changed out of our jungle clothes, and all of us, including little Sara Ximena, Esmeralda's daughter, headed to an outdoor café a few miles from town. We ordered family style and shared soups, chicken, rice, salad and fried *platanos*. Before returning to the house, we stopped by the grocery store in Darien and then, with the late afternoon approaching, returned to Calima so that Margarita, María Isabel and their families could return to Cali before dark. Monday was a school day and they had preparations to make.

Ximena, Rafael and I spent another night at the lake and enjoyed the Jacuzzi in the early evening. After the hectic schedule of the previous week, we were all ready for some quiet time and perhaps some time away from each other. Before going to bed, Ximena and I watched a popular show on TV about Pablo Escobar, and Rafael worked on his computer.

In the week that followed, I gradually realized that I was being a guest of Ximena and Rafael for one week too long. In the same way that all families squabble and annoy each other, we did the same thing and I was ready to leave when the time came – and I'm sure they were ready to resume their normal schedule without having to think about a houseguest. Ximena was protective of me and worried about my safety when I wanted to go out – even when I just wanted to go to the mall. As a result, she would accompany me and then I would feel guilty about taking up her time. I often felt like a prisoner. We continued to do things around town and I was very grateful for their hospitality, but no amount of good will could convince me that I had not stayed too long. By the time my flight finally left, I knew that if I returned to Cali to live, I'd definitely need my own activities and my own apartment.

Soon after I returned to the States, Ximena sent me an email saying that she was making good progress on the translation of *Twice Colombia*. She felt confident it would be popular in Colombia and I was flattered at the thought. I knew nothing about the publication and printing business in Colombia, but set about researching the status and soon realized that, if we went forward with it, I'd have another self-published book. She didn't know how long it would take to complete the project, but indicated that she was working conscientiously. My enthusiasm returned for all things Colombian and memories of a less-than-fulfilling trip had already faded.

Ill winds were blowing, however, and it wouldn't be long before a near-tragedy sent us all reeling.

Chapter Seven

Salomé and the Burro

Roncesvalles, halfway between Cali and Bogotá, is a region of Colombia in the central *cordillera* (mountain range) of the country. At an altitude of approximately 9,500 feet, the temperatures are low, with cool, sunny days and frigid nights. A popular tourist location, people come to this area to enjoy the Colombian pastimes of rest and relaxation. With hiking and horseback riding trails, nature lovers find a special haven. Outdoor music events also attract a lot of people.

For most of the 1990s, guerilla activity in the area was rampant with FARC claiming responsibility for interfering with elections and abducting electoral officials. Among other acts of terrorism, they set fire to public and private properties. They seized voting documents before and after elections and burned them. Bombs were detonated. To fund their activities, they kidnapped many people for ransom, took part in illegal mining, extortion, and the distribution of illegal drugs.

While FARC was creating havoc in this otherwise beautiful and peaceful spot, many Colombians were still traveling in the region. Most had learned how to co-exist with the terrorist culture and took a strong stance when it came to preserving their own way of life. Excursions with their families to favorite areas in the country didn't stop, but of course, precautions were always taken.

It was during this period that several members of my own Colombian family ventured to Roncesvalles for a five-day vacation. María Isabel and her husband Mellizo had bought a *finca* (farm) high in the mountains where they kept horses and cows, and produced a special cheese which they sold in outlets around the country. This was the first time that several family members had been to the *finca* and they were all excited about seeing the new property. Traveling by car, the trip was long and arduous, but spirits were high as they proceeded slowly over the poor roads. They sang and laughed and stopped along the way for a picnic in a grassy field. It wasn't long before they gained altitude and soon pulled out sweaters and jackets to ward off the chilly temperatures.

Arriving late in the afternoon, they were tired but happy, and anxious to get out of the car and move around. They welcomed the roaring fire and hot meal prepared by the couple who cared for the property and took time to tour the barns and pasture before turning in for the evening. After sleeping soundly through a peaceful night, they woke up to a sunny and crisp day that was perfect for a family outing on the grounds of the spacious and prosperous farm. Some of them rode horses and petted the animals and some ate and/or slept most of the day. María Isabel practiced songs on her new guitar, a birthday gift from her husband, Mellizo. It was a glorious day, the kind I remember so vividly about Colombia.

During their second night at the *finca*, while they were sleeping, guerillas stormed into the house, brandishing AK-47s, and terrorized the entire household, including the domestic help. The three men, armed and shouting threats, robbed them of their money and then ordered everyone into a single bedroom and boarded the door, preventing them from escaping. During the night, the men ate the food that was in the house and took turns sleeping on the floor by the warm fireplace. My friends were terrified, but unharmed. As soon as the sun rose, the intruders allowed them to quickly gather their belongings and flee the premises.

It was an event that kept my family away from the *finca* for many years. Eventually, some of the men returned, but it would be still longer before they felt it was safe enough to take the women and children again – and none of the women wanted to go. Approximately fifteen years later, however, the entire family returned to the *finca* where they again rode horses during the day and slept peacefully at night - no guerillas in sight. Things were improving in Colombia.

In December, 2012, several family members, now with children of their own who were not at the *finca* when it was stormed by the guerillas, traveled to Roncesvalles for the Christmas holidays. Their days were filled with horseback riding, hiking, music and resting in the hammocks. The younger children in the group spent time with the smaller animals – dogs, cats and burros. The youngest of the group, Salomé, had become attached to one of the burros and had no fear of him. She was seven years old and went up to him easily and lovingly and claimed him as her own pet.

One morning she approached the small animal with the intention of petting him on his head. Perhaps she startled him. In retaliation he lunged at her and ripped open her scalp with his teeth. The skin was pulled back from the front to the crown of her head and, as she raised her hand to protect herself, he also bit her hand and arm in several places, fracturing a finger. Her blood-curdling screams pierced the tranquil morning, bringing family members, horrified, frantically to her side. Fortunately, Mellizo, who is an orthopedic surgeon, was in the yard at the time and immediately came to her rescue. He wrapped her injuries with cloths and told Ricardo, her father, to get the car for a trip to the hospital. With Salomé going into shock from the loss of so much blood, they were quickly off for what is usually a twenty minute trip in the best of circumstances. By the time they arrived at the small clinic, thirty minutes later, Salomé was unresponsive. With Mellizo leading the activity, they were able to stabilize her vital signs and prepare for surgery. Forty-four stitches were needed to close the wound on her scalp and several others for the lacerations on her arm and hand.

She survived the attack, and with skilled care, improved quickly. Mellizo, however, didn't allow her to make the trip back to Cali for a week because of the bumpy roads and the fear of hemorrhaging, but as soon as she was able to travel she returned to the city and began therapy to regain use of her right hand. Children are usually resilient and Ximena wrote that Salomé didn't complain much about the scalp wound, but did feel limited by the injuries to her hand since she was right-handed. Family members provided round-the-clock care and gave thanks every day that the injury had not been more severe.

By the end of January, Salomé had improved considerably and life was getting back to normal for her and her family. I relisted my house at a lower price and decided that I would give it six more months and if no buyer appeared, I would have no choice but to take it off the market and forget about making a move to Colombia. The constant uncertainty was becoming stressful and I was tired of being so unsettled. My special renewable visa, which had been time-consuming and expensive to obtain, had just arrived. It would enable me to stay in Colombia for a year at a time and I tucked it away in a drawer, thinking that maybe I wouldn't need it after all.

Ximena wrote that she had found a reputable publisher in Cali for the book, now called *Dos Veces en Colombia,* and she offered to help broker a good and fair deal. I made contact with the business, but realized that it would be very difficult to accomplish anything through emails, especially since there was a language barrier. I started thinking about another short trip to Colombia to take care of the business end of this project and I continued to prepare for a possible move.

Roncesvalles

Chapter Eight

Buying and Selling Within
24 Hours, 2013

Activity in the housing market picked up, and while I had always had showings in the past, I was encouraged by the increased number of people who wanted to see the house. One couple in particular appeared more interested than others. While they (and others) were looking and discussing the pros and cons, I continued to prepare for a move. I located a storage facility to place the furniture I planned to keep, if I decided to move. I called a mover for quotes. There was a special hotel in town that catered to people with temporary housing needs, and I thought it would be a perfect place for me to stay for a couple of weeks while waiting to finalize the house closing – if there was one - and last minute details. The manager offered me a reasonable deal. But, until the house was sold, these were just items on my list of things to do.

My stress level increased and I had moments when I wondered if it was all worth it. Yoga and walking helped keep me focused and as calm as possible. Most stressful of all was dealing with a computer that probably needed a good update and the constant worry about taking care of financial matters on the Internet if I were in Colombia. I imagined the worst case scenarios. It could never be as simple as it was back in the 70s and 80s, and I was well aware of that. Kelly called one day and said a couple wanted to come back for a second look at the house.

"I think they're really interested, Patricia. His parents live close by and the wife works at home with a computer business. The wife's mother also lives with them and the two separate living areas in your house would be perfect for them."

"Great! I'll clean the bathrooms and check the fresh flowers. Thanks, Kelly," I said. It had been nearly two years since I showed my house the first time and I had learned how to quickly make things presentable. In the beginning, it was always exciting to know that someone was coming to look at this house which I had so lovingly cared for. Even when there was no follow up, I felt optimistic, knowing that I was still committed to making this dream of moving to Colombia again come true. Or so I thought.

That night, Kelly called and said, "Patricia, everything went great at the showing and they want to send an electrician to the house to make sure that the wiring will support their computer needs. I've already called Romero's (a local electrician who, coincidentally, was originally from Cali, Colombia) and he can be there tomorrow morning at 10 a.m. if that's convenient."

"That's perfect. I'll plan to leave by 9:45."

"Okay, I'll meet the couple and the electrician at 10 and I'll call you when we're finished." Kelly always impressed me with her conscientiousness and competence and today was no exception. I felt lucky to have her on my side.

Two hours after the electrical inspection the next day, Kelly called to say that, in spite of the age of the house, no serious issues were found. Within a few days, the couple made an offer and negotiations began in earnest. A professional home inspection was done, and the couple came back several times to look at different aspects of the house. They walked around the yard, went inside the newly re-sided shed in the backyard and asked about the rain-water barrel I had placed under an eave. I told them I planned to leave it. There was an old greenhouse on the property which I had used to store gardening tools and supplies, and I could tell that the young man was interested in horticulture. He especially liked the pergola which Larry had built not long after I moved in and they admired the hanging ferns. I pointed out the camellias and dogwoods and the many different azalea plants in the back yard and mentioned the spring flowers which had already bloomed. We looked at the gardenias which bordered the back deck and noted that they were full of buds. Their sweet summertime smell would linger a few months on into the fall. A couple of magnolia trees and a few hollies would serve them well during the Christmas season. The acuba bushes would supply them with year-round greenery. Apparently, the deer didn't have a taste for the plants in my yard, but a couple of them had once bolted across the deck knocking over all of my herbs that were in pots. Occasionally, I would open the back door and see them grazing in an empty lot next door. When I told the prospective buyer about the fox that sometimes passed through, his eyes lit up. The birds, squirrels, and sometimes turtles and snakes, were also very much a part of the landscape.

At some point in their exploration, I started thinking that maybe it was truly going to happen this time. *Maybe* I'd give up ownership of this place that I'd loved so much and held so close to my heart for eleven years. I was beginning to feel a sense of loss and separation anxiety already. I'd heard about seller's remorse, but never imagined I'd fall in that category. A part of me wanted to stop the entire process and never let go of something that meant so much to me. Another more reasonable part of me prevailed, and I concentrated on thinking about what it would eventually mean to me to no longer have the responsibility of the house.

With a decision on the house expected soon, the proverbial straw that broke the camel's back splintered at my desk one day. My computer crashed, and, instead of panicking, I very quietly turned it off, and took a deep breath. In a sense, it was almost a relief, because I knew I couldn't move forward with plans to move to Colombia with my computer inaccessible. So many aspects of my life were dependent on the Internet, that, in a split second, I made the decision to take the profit from the sale of my house, if it sold, and buy a small condominium in New Bern. After that, I could decide about Colombia.

Kelly helped me find one on the water in Riverbend, a residential area a few miles outside of town. That was where Jamie and I lived for a few years after he arrived in the States. The one I chose needed work, but had great potential and with the profit I finally made on my house, I was able to pay cash for the condo and have enough left over for renovations. I closed on both places a day apart and put plans to move to Colombia on hold. My computer was repaired and my stress level went down.

Making the decision to buy the condominium was one of the best I'd ever made. I knew that as soon as I got settled, I'd be able to travel again without worry about the care of my house. With no mortgage payment life would be much simpler and I slept well knowing that Colombia would always be a part of my life, just not in the way I had previously envisioned.

Six months after buying the condo, I was on my way back to Colombia to finalize plans for the publication of *Twice Colombia* in Spanish. Ximena and Esteban made it possible to finally work out a deal with the publisher and all that was left to do was choose a date for the book launch. It was now February, 2014, and I was given a choice of April or June for the event, to be held at the National Library in Cali. I chose June since Ximena was scheduled for back surgery and I wanted to make sure that, as the translator, she would be well enough to attend and be recognized. It was a short trip and without the worry about my house, I was able to enjoy my friends and Cali as much as ever.

A few days before I was scheduled to return back to the States, Esteban called and asked if I'd like to go to Piedechinche, the restored sugar cane plantation and museum. I hadn't been there since the 1980s and always hoped I'd be able to go back some day.

"A former high school classmate of mine is the resident veterinarian there and I called him to see if we could visit," Esteban said. "Do you want to go?"

"I'd love to! That would be a perfect way to end the trip," I said. I didn't know there were enough animals there to justify a full-time veterinarian, but I found out later there are twenty-five horses on the property.

After an early morning drive to the museum the next day, with Esteban and Marta both talking on their individual phones, we met Miguel in his office and enjoyed coffee while he and Esteban caught up on old times. Marta didn't know him in high school but she had met him at events over the years. I couldn't understand much of what they were saying, but I understood the friendship and the connection they had to their high school days. They made an effort to include me in everything they said and somehow I knew the comfortable feeling of being with old friends.

After walking through the lush and beautiful gardens with a guide and then touring the inside of the house, we returned to Miguel's office where he was waiting for us. There was some chatting and then discussion about lunch and soon we were in Miguel's well-used SUV riding through the hot and dusty countryside. Miguel and Esteban sat in the front, and Marta and I in the back.

We arrived at the little town of Santa Elena shortly after 1 p.m. and found a parking space in front of an open-air restaurant where Miguel often ate. With four or five tables and the kitchen in plain view, and two employees scurrying around, the restaurant was airy and shaded in the midday heat. Miguel spoke to the women when we walked in and they answered in kind. A tantalizing aroma filled the room as we chose a table and sat down in old, wooden chairs.

Within minutes, one of the waitresses brought us a cool and refreshing drink made from *panela* (sugar cane), water and lemon. It was light and sweet. There was a choice of chicken or beef for the main dish and I opted for the chicken. Ordering a meal in a place like this was always an adventure. Usually the cooks prepared whatever was available and it did no good to ask too many questions. It was enough for me that

Miguel recommended it. Soon, we were served huge bowls of a steaming beef and vegetable soup which even Miguel and Esteban were not able to finish. It would have been sufficient for my entire meal, but I knew from experience there would be more. My main dish arrived with a beautifully roasted half-chicken, rice, beans, a salad of cucumbers, carrots and cabbage, and a slice of sweet *platano* for dessert. I ate slowly and deliberately and found it hard to concentrate on the conversation. Miguel spoke even less English than I spoke Spanish, but with Esteban's and Marta's help we managed to communicate. He did ask where I was from and when I told him New Bern, North Carolina, on the coast, he wanted to know if it was the Pacific or Atlantic coast. So much for thinking North Carolina is the center of the universe. We savored every bite that we took and finished the meal with contentment. When the bill came it was about $4(US) per person. I wondered what it would be like to live in a small town like Santa Elena in Colombia. Before leaving we asked one of the employees to take a picture of the four of us in front of the restaurant with a view of a vegetable and fruit stall behind us. We then slowly ambled to the car and climbed back in.

On the short drive back to Piedechinche, I told Miguel that I had some pictures taken at the museum in 1982 when I visited Cali with the Friendship Force. If he wanted, I could send copies when I returned home. He seemed happy to hear that and I made plans to try to locate them as soon as I could.

In Santa Elena with Miguel, Marta and Esteban.

On the late afternoon drive back into the city, I sat in the front of the car with Esteban, and Marta sat in the back. We were relaxed and comfortable. We talked a little about things in general and suddenly Esteban said, "Patricia, when did Jamie die?"

"It was April 1, 2001," I replied. "I can always remember the date because it was the same year of the terrorist attack on the World Trade Center." I wasn't really surprised that he asked the question, but it was unexpected. However, Esteban and all my friends in Cali knew that I felt comfortable talking about Jamie, and I always felt they were being considerate whenever they brought up his name by offering me a chance to talk about him if I wanted.

Esteban continued, "I remember when he was a little boy and the two of you would come to the pizzeria and he always had a huge appetite. I've never seen a child eat that much." I laughed because it was very true. Even after he'd been with me for a while and had had his fill he still ate, at times, as if he were starving. I always thought the memory of the hunger and deprivation he had experienced before being taken to the orphanage would probably never leave him.

"Yes, we had some good times in Cali. He loved going to school and taking part in all the activities. He liked going to the pool and getting in the water, but he was scared of it for a long time. It wasn't until after we returned to the States that he really learned how to swim, and once he did, I couldn't keep him out of the water." We laughed again and I remembered trips to the North and South Carolina beaches and how he wanted to bury himself in the sand on his first trip to Bear Island. We had a lot of fun exploring the area after he arrived.

"How old was he," asked Marta, "when you adopted him? I remember that he was very small for his age."

"He was six when I first met him and seven when he came to live with me. By the time he actually arrived in the States he was eight. And, you're right, he was small. I never imagined he would turn into the strapping six-foot-three man that he became."

"So, he was twenty-three when he died?" Esteban asked.

"Yes, twenty-three," I replied. "We had some very good years together and then, everything changed."

Jamie - Irony

There's something ironic about adopting a child from a foreign country, thoroughly convinced you'll be able to provide him a safe and good life, only to lose him in the end to the very violence from which you were sure you were protecting him.

April 1, 2001, didn't start off as any other Sunday morning. Relishing a few extra hours of rest, I usually slept until 7:30 or 8:00 and then enjoyed a leisurely breakfast before reading the paper and then starting whatever projects I might have on my agenda that day. On that Sunday morning, however, I was jolted awake at 6:00 a.m. with a sense that something was wrong. I bolted upright, wide awake, alert, and listened. There were no unusual sounds, no smell of smoke, no storm or hurricane brewing, no birds singing. All was eerily quiet. The early morning light was enough for me to see my way to the kitchen where I started a pot of coffee, and then pulled back the curtains on the sliding glass door which opened to the patio and backyard. "A few of these majestic pine trees need to come down," I thought, as I lingered at the view, and smiled at how I'd always loved the woods, forests, jungles, anything green from Mother Nature. If it were possible, I'd live in a tree. I loved my backyard and smiled at the pleasure I felt knowing that this little plot of land was mine.

After walking outside and picking up the newspapers and noticing the overcast skies, I returned to the house where I dropped the papers beside my favorite chair in the living room. The gray morning and cool temperature, along with a good night's sleep, put me in a mellow, nesting mood which didn't happen often, but when it did, I always wanted to do quiet things like sewing or embroidery. Eventually, I repaired a hem in a skirt and sewed on a button and somehow felt comforted by the simple acts.

After breakfast, a shower, and skimming the newspapers, I pulled out my school work and spread the papers and books on the dining room table. The end of the grading period was near and there was a lot of make-up work to evaluate before I could average grades and then prepare lesson plans for the coming week. By ten a.m., I was making good progress and thinking that I might finish in time to go to a movie in the afternoon.

At 10:30, the doorbell rang. My first thought was how unusual that was. People didn't ordinarily go visiting on Sunday mornings and it was unexpected. I didn't think beyond that. I tried to stay focused on a test I was grading as I walked to the kitchen door. Glancing through the window, I saw a police car in the driveway. That would not have been unusual had Jamie been living at home, but he was now in Wilmington and the local police would have no reason to come to my house now. Then, I saw two police officers, a man and a woman, and my neighbor, Mrs. Jones, dressed in her housecoat. I opened the door and stared at them. Mrs. Jones gently pushed me aside and came in, followed by the two officers, who looked serious but kind. I must have moved, but I don't remember. Someone guided me to the sofa and sat me down and then one of the policemen said, "Ms. Woodard, I'm very sorry to inform you that your son, James, who lives in Wilmington, has been declared a homicide victim." I remember staring, thinking he was telling me that Jamie had been in an accident. Homicide. Victim. It didn't register for a moment.

As I started to respond by asking if he was okay, the meaning of what he said seeped in, and fear and shock filled my body and mind. I must have been staring at him with a questioning look because he said, "Yes, it happened about 5:00 a.m. this morning and he was pronounced dead at the hospital at 6:00 a.m. Apparently, it was a drug deal gone bad."

He continued to talk and asked for my sister's phone number. The second officer called her while the first one called the officer in Wilmington who was in charge of the investigation. I listened to him for a few minutes and

123

confirmed that I had talked to Jamie on the phone the previous Wednesday night and that we had plans to meet on the following Saturday. He asked about what to do with the body and I told him that Cotton Funeral Home in New Bern would handle arrangements. Other things may have been discussed, but I don't remember. The tears didn't come quickly, but they came, quietly and painfully, with each one searing my heart.

Soon, my sister Rachel arrived, and then my principal, Greg Williams, with one of the assistant principals, Terry Fuhrman. As Greg gave me a hug, I said "Our children aren't supposed to go before we do."

"I know," he answered, and offered comfort and condolences from a loving place in his soul.

Others arrived and soon there were phone calls from family and close friends who lived out of town. Reverend Singleton, our neighbor from across the street, was notified by Mrs. Jones and he came immediately. A representative from the funeral home came by, and I found the information about a life insurance policy I had bought for Jamie right after we arrived in the States. Rachel and I set a time to visit the funeral home later that afternoon to arrange the service.

I decided to have his body cremated, and when we went to the funeral home at 4:30 p.m., I asked if I might see him before the cremation took place. I didn't realize an autopsy had already been done, so because of that, I was told that I couldn't. That was when I felt my first heaving sob and it didn't stop until we left the funeral home thirty minutes later. I felt depleted and weak and wanted only to get home. When night came, after hours spent pacing the floor, perhaps in an attempt to stay busy in order to avoid thinking about what had happened, I insisted that Rachel go to her own home, asking only that she stay until I had a shower. I knew I would be okay by myself.

The next day, the house filled up quickly as friends and family came to pay their respects. Rachel was the first to come back and soon Mother, my sister Sara and her husband, Jerry, arrived from Whiteville. Mother stayed in my house with me, and Sara and Jerry stayed in a nearby motel. A close cousin, Larry Dunnagan, from Myrtle Beach, who would be my escort at the funeral, arrived after lunch. He was staying at Rachel's house.

The decision to have the funeral on Tuesday was made on the spur of the moment, and later, I regretted thinking that I had to do it so soon. I suppose I was thinking that being efficient and decisive were important at that time. They weren't. More time absorbing the shock of what had happened would probably have been more beneficial than feeling I was in control and had taken care of matters in a timely and responsible manner.

The visitation was on Monday evening and many friends and family who would not be able to attend the funeral came that night. Their presence was comforting and a few people came with stories to tell about Jamie which were funny and uplifting. I feel like I floated in a hazy mist through that gathering because I remember so little about it.

My feelings about the funeral are the same and perhaps that's a blessing. There were people close by who wanted to support and care for me, and eventually, I let them do it. They were patient and non-judgmental and never blamed me or criticized Jamie. They were just there with love and concern. The days passed slowly as I took each new step and tried not to let myself think about too many things. My soul needed healing and there were dark days to get through.

After a week, and after cleaning out Jamie's apartment in Wilmington, I went back to work. Easter vacation was coming soon and there would be time to sort through things at home and reassess this huge change in my life later. After seventeen years, my boy was gone.

Jamie and Patricia in Wilmington, a few months before his death.

Chapter Nine

Book Launch in Cali, 2014

Soon after my return from Cali in February, 2014, when Esteban, Marta and I talked about Jamie on the way back from Piedechinche, Ximena had her back surgery which was successful. While she was recovering right on schedule, I was glad I had chosen to have the book launch in late June instead of April. I wanted her to be there and receive recognition for her part in bringing this work to life, as the translator, and she needed time to heal. The translation was not perfect, and she was distraught, but once the book was published, there was no going back. I knew that well from my own experiences with the first publication in English, and tried to reassure her that the errors would not distract from the story. Also, she didn't need the stress of worrying about something that couldn't be changed, and frankly, I was just ready to get it done.

My high school friend Linda Hufham, who had visited me in New Bern when *Twice Colombia* was first published, decided to come with me on this trip, and I was delighted to have a chance to share my adopted country with her. She had never traveled in South America and was curious, as well as hesitant. Most people who visit Colombia the first time feel that way. Even though I did my best to describe a country that was warm and loving and welcoming in the book *Twice Colombia*, most of my friends and acquaintances, and especially family, in the

States weren't convinced. Of course, there were considerations in preparing for the trip, but none of the obstacles were insurmountable. I wanted Linda to be prepared. Clothing, for example, was a main issue. Any items that might bring undue attention to oneself should be left at home. There's no better example of that than the red *ruana* incident in Bogotá in 1975. After that, I took all of these recommendations more seriously and tried to convey that to anyone who asked. The objective is to disappear as much as possible into the crowd. So, that means no flashy jewelry, no revealing clothes, and no loud or rude gestures. Being fashionably dressed should not be an objective when out in public because it might draw attention from the wrong sources. Adopting that frame of mind will not detract from the discovery of a different culture nor will it prevent one from enjoying the many pleasures to be found there. So, with all of that advice, Linda bravely took on the challenge of traveling to Colombia.

We met in Miami on June 23, 2014, after I nearly missed my connection. My flight from Charlotte arrived on time, but we couldn't deplane because of a storm with lightning and 20K winds. As soon as the weather cleared and we were allowed to leave, I ran to the next boarding gate and watched the attendants close the doors. I pleaded with them to let me in and, by the grace of God, they did. I made it just in time, but my luggage didn't.

On the trip to Cali, Linda and I enjoyed the superb service of Avianca, the Colombian airlines. I had sung their praises for so long that I felt a personal pride in being able to share it finally with someone from home. We talked and laughed and reminisced about high school days and, of course, past boyfriends. We talked about my lack of a decision regarding a move to Colombia and how my feelings about the move were changing. I was having trouble making up my mind. Linda and I covered a lot of territory during those three and one-half hours.

Marta, Esteban and Sofía met us at the airport and took us to our hotel, *Stancia Spiwak*, where I had stayed on my previous trip. Fortunately, I had packed survival items in my carry-on bag and by the time I got up the next morning, my luggage had arrived.

After a plentiful, complimentary breakfast the next morning, and lunch with Esteban at Chipichape mall, the city nearly shut down as Italy and Uruguay played in a soccer match. Uruguay won and people left their televisions and headed back outside. Colombia was playing on Friday and the country was getting ready for all the hoopla. President Juan Manuel Santos had already declared Friday a "dry" day with no alcohol to be sold in stores or restaurants for a 24-hour period. People in Colombia really take their soccer seriously.

On Wednesday, the day of the book launch, Ximena came to the hotel and picked up Linda and me for lunch, and then we returned to the hotel to rest and get dressed for the evening program. This was one time when it was acceptable to be a little dressed up because we would be in a group in the State library and would be taken there in a private car. I had chosen what I called a "Michelle Obama" style dress because I wanted to show that I was still a proud North American and I thought the choice was flattering and pretty. Black and white, with a fitted waist and full skirt (with built-in crinoline), scooped neckline and hitting just above the knee: it reminded me of a classic 1950s style. A bright salmon-colored thin belt placed it in the 21st century. I covered my bare arms with a sheer, cropped, black, Ann Taylor sweater. I even chose to wear a strand of pearls which had been a gift from my parents many years ago along with pearl drop earrings. This was definitely their (the pearls) first trip to Colombia! With high heels and a clutch bag, I looked anything but the traveling, vagabond, visitor. Esteban whistled when I stepped out of the elevator and complimented me on my dress. I said *"El estilo de Michelle Obama"* (Michelle Obama's style) and he indicated that, yes, he liked her style.

I had prepared my speech very carefully a few months earlier and had practiced it in Spanish until I nearly had it memorized. Ximena did the translation and I was ready to express to a roomful of strangers, within 10 minutes or less, my inspiration for writing the book. Two other authors who had written about the Cauca Valley, where Cali is located, were being recognized that night and I was the first one to give my presentation. When I looked out at the group, I recognized a few faces and saw nearly forty years flash before my eyes. This is what I said, in Spanish:

"Thank you, and good evening ladies and gentlemen. I am very honored to be here tonight.

Nearly forty years ago, when I first stepped foot on Colombian soil, a young woman full of curiosity and a desire to see the world, never in my wildest dreams did I imagine that I was embarking on a journey that would turn into the odyssey of a lifetime. That journey, in time, was given a name, when my book, *Twice Colombia*, was published in English, and now, *Dos Veces en Colombia*, in Spanish.

People have always asked me how it happened that I came to Colombia. After all, in 1975, the main news out of the country involved drug cartels, crime and terrorism, earthquakes and a corrupt government. Why would anybody want to go to a place like that? When I tried to explain, I realized that answering that question would take more than a few sentences and the only way I could tell the whole story would be to write it down and hope that I could remember enough to be fair and honest in sharing my recollections.

My sister Rachel, when she found out I had accepted a teaching position in a private school in Bogotá, said all she could visualize about Colombia were women with baskets of fruit on their heads. And I'll admit that, at that time, in 1975, the country was somewhat of a mystery to me, too. On my first day in Bogotá, I looked around the El Dorado airport and took in the smells, the sounds, and the people, and the one thing I didn't see was women with baskets of fruit on their heads. I was visually jolted by the cosmopolitan and sophisticated people: the men with their aura of healthy pride and the women, in particular, who wore their aristocratic bearing in the same way they wore their smooth and chocolatey-textured boots, their professionally styled hairdos and their plush, soft, woolen *ruanas* – confidently and comfortably. That was not what I expected.

While my first stay in Colombia was not long, it opened my eyes to a culture that was accomplished and proud and very different from what I was accustomed to. I also discovered the lighter side with *pan de bono, tinto, fincas, ajiaco*, DAS, the Amazon, Colombian dances and music, *aguardiente* and the luxury of having a live-in-maid, and I was very grateful for the experience.

While the title of my book, *Twice Colombia*, is described as a story of adventure, friendship and adoption in the Andes Mountains, and it certainly is all of those things, a more accurate description might be "a love letter to Colombia," because over time, after many trips, I did fall in love with the country and the people. Like an infatuated adolescent, I chose not to dwell on the faults and shortcomings of the object of my affection in the beginning. Time, however, provided me a wider perspective as I watched the country and its people suffer, and then, get back on its feet with resounding strength. Our relationship came full circle.

Thanks to an organization known as the Friendship Force of North Carolina, I returned to Colombia six years later, to the city of Cali, which seemed to me at the time to be in a different country than Bogotá. While Bogotá had its charms, Cali was altogether a different place. The weather was delightful, there was no need for heavy clothes, people smiled and were friendly, and most importantly, I was placed in the home of a loving and caring Colombian family. During that 10-day trip, we visited the sugarcane plantation and museum, Piedechinche, the Indian community of Sylvia where the purple and pink native clothes were handmade and unique, Popayan, the home of many of Colombia's famous artists and writers, Lake Calima, where my Colombian family has vacationed for decades, and Los Farrallones, the national park where we went for all day outings, cooking, eating, resting and swimming in the river. I tasted *sancocho*, *empanadas* and *arepas* for the first time and listened to Roberto Carlos. I discovered a rich and vibrant culture all because my host family knew there was value in sharing their lives with someone from a different culture. The trip flew by quickly, but not before I visited a few schools and picked up applications for teaching positions. Fortunately, not long after the Friendship Force trip, I was offered a job at Colegio Bolívar and returned to Cali as soon as I could to begin the second part of my journey in this beautiful country. My Colombian friends, as well as my colleagues at Colegio Bolívar, were always available, and with the generosity and support of both groups, I felt welcomed unconditionally to the country.

I learned that we all probably have more in common with foreign cultures than we sometimes acknowledge. The Colombians I have met over the years are kind, gentle and loving people who want the same things for their families and loved ones as we all do. They have always treated me with respect and fairness and I hope that I've done the same. They also have a wonderful sense of humor. I truly hope that my book expresses my belief that understanding between people of different cultures can take place if we are willing to listen to each other's life experiences.

In closing, I could spend the rest of the evening talking about my Colombian family and what they have meant to me, but suffice it to say, I'm here now, after all these many years later, celebrating the publication of this book, because of them. To my first host family, Esteban Plata and Marta Rivas, Rafael Franco and Ximena Plata, my translator, your children, brothers and sisters and nieces and nephews and now your grandchildren, thank you. You have enriched my life beyond measure. I love you and I love Colombia.

Thank you."

There was applause and cheering and I guess the audience understood my Spanish. Linda said they all laughed at the right places so that was a good indication. There was a short question and answer period before the second author presented, and I was assisted by Rafael, Ximena's husband, who had a good command of the English language.

A man stood up and thanked me, in Spanish, for coming to Colombia and writing so kindly about the country. "We are not accustomed to such praise. Thank you again."

Another person commented on the fact that I did not address, in detail, the political situation and perhaps I should have. After discussion with Rafael, I simply said, "I don't feel qualified to speak about that. This story is about families and cultures and I'll leave the politics to those more knowledgeable." That seemed to satisfy him and then one more person spoke.

"Patricia, when are you coming back here to live? I think you would like to live here, no?"

"Very much," I replied. "There are complications and visa issues and many things to consider. But, thank you, I hope that I can."

"Well," he responded, "please hurry, we're waiting for you."

With that comment, I knew I'd be back. How could I not after a suggestion like that from a total stranger? Maybe not as a permanent resident in the way I had thought for so long, but as someone who was lucky enough to have known Colombia in a very special way and would always know Colombia, whether in the States or in the land of *El Dorado*. All the worry and concerns about housing and computers could be dealt with and I would return at this special time in my life, in my own special way, grateful for the gift I received.

After the launch and a celebratory dinner with the Platas and Francos in a Middle Eastern restaurant, Linda and I wrapped up our week with visits to some of my favorite places in the area: Sylvia, Popayan, Piedechinche, La Loma de la Cruz, El Paloma and the mall Chipichape, where we did some serious shopping. I was beginning to feel like a tour guide and loving every minute of it. We ate *empanadas, pan de bono* and had our fill of fresh fruit. I think Linda understood how I felt about my Colombian friends, and before we left, she was in love with them and they with her. She was curious about FARC and ELN, two guerilla groups, and on the way to Sylvia, Rafael pointed out areas where they often tried to cross the highway at night on their way to Buenaventura and the coast. Soldiers were always in that area, sometimes hiding out of sight, and she saw plenty of them. Rafael continued to raise his thumb in support as we passed groups of them, and I found myself now doing the same thing. I was glad they were there.

Celebrating with my Colombian family after the book launch in Cali.

Before leaving Colombia, we stopped in Bogotá for a few days and were lucky to have reservations in the *Candelaria* area which was a wonderful place to walk and visit museums and art galleries in the daytime. We walked and ate and slept soundly at night. It was a fulfilling visit, and I was delighted to finally share it with a friend from home. The night before we left Bogotá, we heard news on the TV about a hurricane that was expected to move up the east coast of the United States the next day. Moaning and dreading the possible inconveniences, we went to bed thinking about the disruptions that occur in airports when hurricanes come through.

When we arrived in Miami, flights were being rerouted and canceled and we parted ways hoping to make our own connections with the fewest possible problems. Linda was going to Atlanta, and I was headed to Charlotte before the final leg into New Bern. It didn't take long to realize that there would be some changes, and as it turned out, my flight into Charlotte was delayed and I would have missed the next flight into New Bern if it had not been canceled. Fortunately, I was able to get a room at a hotel in Charlotte for the night and arrived home safely the next day, giving thanks again for a carefully packed carry-on bag.

The story would have ended there with much gratitude for a fulfilling trip and a sense that I knew where my Colombian story was headed next, but while I was at the hotel in Charlotte, I received a friends request on Facebook from a Dean Gonyea. I didn't know a Dean Gonyea, but I once had a dear friend at Colegio Nueva Granada in 1975-76 whose name was Jerry Gonyea. We had explored Bogotá and traveled together while making the most of our stay in Colombia's capital. He was my partner on an unforgettable trip down the Amazon. My attempts to locate him when I was writing *Twice Colombia* had been futile. Could this person possibly be connected to that Jerry? It didn't take long to find out that yes, it was the same person and our emails soon sailed across the Internet. Where could this next chapter possibly lead? I had thought I'd be able to loosen the ties to Colombia with the publication of *Twice Colombia* in Spanish, but this new development could change everything. With happy anticipation, I returned to my life in

New Bern and started making plans for my next visit to my beloved Colombia. If Jerry and I reconnected perhaps we could travel together again. He was the best traveling companion ever and that was just what I needed then. My Colombian friends were irreplaceable but they weren't always able to travel when I was able to go. This could change everything.

Epilogue

As I finish this story, I'm on a three-month trip to Cali, Colombia, with plans to finish this second book and to develop an idea for a children's book about cultural diversity. My friend Esteban found a small furnished apartment for me, *Cora Suites*, in the Granada section of the city and it has been an ideal location and environment. A little noisy at times, it offers diversity and a comfortable nest for me to do my work. I love being able to walk around and visit the many restaurants, and of course, my Colombian friends are close by. Only recently did I realize that the orphanage where Jamie spent a few months before I adopted him, is just a couple of blocks away. I think about that a lot when I'm out walking in the neighborhood, and realize that his story is what this second book is really about. With maid service six days a week and breakfast served in my room, I have no excuse for not finding the time to be productive. The staff here at the hotel are accommodating and anxious to please. The maids practice their English with me and I continue to practice my Spanish. They've helped spruce up my apartment by bringing in a small rug and several kitchen utensils I need. Occasionally they'll bring extra fruit. They tiptoe around me very quietly when I'm working at the computer and stop their chattering if they know I'm busy. I've signed up for Tango lessons at *Tango Vivo y Salsa Viva* and am looking forward to getting away from the computer with that diversion twice a week.

After a month spent settling in, I am now waiting for my friend Jerry's arrival in a few days for a week-long visit. During the last several months, we've had the opportunity to get to know each other again and renew our friendship. The feelings I had about him nearly forty years ago were confirmed when he told me he had been in two serious relationships over the years and that he was gay. Fortunately for him, he has been open about it for many years and lives in a state that openly supports the gay community. None of that, however, has affected our friendship. I accept him as he is and am thrilled that we are going to make another connection. My Colombian friends here understand that he is not a boyfriend, but I haven't told them yet that he is gay. They may already suspect it from the things I've said, but I will confirm that soon. I'm curious to know what their reaction will be.

We have plans to see everything we can in Cali and the surrounding area and will spend the weekend at Lake Calima with my family. If we had more time I'm sure we'd be doing some exotic traveling, but this time, with just a few days, there probably won't be any skinny-dipping in the Amazon again, just reminiscing about some long ago fun times - but I'm not ruling out anything else. Who knows, maybe we'll both feel the pull to come back and settle in again. Or maybe we'll accept that Colombia will always be our muse, and whether our lives are pulsing with life or death, some beats will always be in the land of *El Dorado*.

Printed in the United States
by Baker & Taylor Publisher Services

Printed in the United States
By Bookmasters